Your Lighthouse Journey
Guided Wisdom in Motion

Dirk Sanden

Dedication

This book is dedicated to everyone who wonders whether there is more to life than just salary payments, TPS reports, and the daily commute.

It is written for the people who are convinced that most of their fundamental questions in life can be answered by applying common sense.

It is specially created for those who are seeking an answer on how to turn common sense into common practice.

Acknowledgment

First of all, a round of applause to my fantastic family & friends for being a pool of support when the writing was driest, and my rowdiest cheerleaders when my head was above water.

Special thanks to my wife, Fadila. Without her constant support and a relentless search for personal development, it wouldn't be the book that you are holding in your hands right now.

Thanks also to my wonderful editors who whipped this book into shape.

And lastly, I thank you, the readers. I hope my book helps you to look at your lives from a new perspective.

When we just stop and appreciate everything in this

PERFECT PRESENT MOMENT.

When we stop seeking an endpoint and

instead, make each moment an end in itself.

When we can appreciate THE JOURNEY

so much that the destination is not needed,

THE JOURNEY IS THE NEW DESTINATION.

Fearless Soul

Preface
Introduction To My
Lighthouse Journey

It is the summer break of 2018, and I find myself sitting in the living room of my mother's place up in the North of Germany. The country and the rest of Europe is hit by a heatwave. It doesn't often happen that we reach a temperature of 38 degrees centigrade (around 100 degrees Fahrenheit) in these lines of latitude, but this year, both literally figuratively – the heat is on!

My story of awakening actually started just before I turned 47 in September of 2015. I got closer to the magical age of 50 and, maybe this, together with a feeling of emptiness, triggered a discussion with my wife. Obviously, I didn't leave the best impression back then and instead of living my life to the best possible, I looked like a dead man walking. Wise as my wife is, she raised a couple of valid questions. These were the questions that I didn't dare to ask myself; questions that kicked-off something big in my life. At the same time, the voice in the back of my head was getting louder with each passing day. This voice continued asking questions as if the baton was passed on from my wife. Questions like: How much money did they pay me to give up on my dreams? Why don't I feel fulfilled and happy despite the fact that I have played according to the rules of the society, achieved a nice career with excellent salary, pension rights, and a reputable social status? What will people say about me at my funeral? What is the deeper meaning of purpose, and why is a purpose crucial for living an abundant life? Last but not least, provided that we can agree on the fact that all of the above questions can be (at least to a certain extent) answered by applying common sense, what holds us back so persistently to turn the answers into common practice?

I was confused as I lead (from a social standpoint) a successful life. Materially, I had all what they told me it would be. But this little voice reminded me that it was not everything that I knew it could be. So, I found myself with a nice little patchwork family, a nice house, nice cars and a motorbike in one of the wealthiest countries of the globe. And yet, there was this vacuum; a feeling of emptiness. And at that point in time, my unconscious wish for more took shape. Still unclear about what "more" meant, I struggled to find my way to satisfying answers. I already had a vague idea. Now I was looking for something more fulfilling and purposeful, something that followed my heart and my passion. Something that had a higher value and was more important than me and my personal, material well-being.

I was born in Bremerhaven, a city in Germany near the Northern Sea, and that probably explains my personal affinity for lighthouses. It was a city with a pulse that was driven by the tides. A city that was dependent over centuries on fishing and hard work in the harbour. It was also a city that ranked pretty high in terms of unemployment rate and pretty low in terms of life changing opportunities.

My father was an engineer. He was working as a chief of the engine room on freight liners. My mother was working as a shop assistant and she took good care of my older brother, my sister and me in a village located between Bremerhaven and Bremen, while my father was crossing oceans. We were a middle class family. We had everything that we needed and we learned the rules of our society well. We were told to keep both feet on the ground, to do what was necessary to get a good job, earn enough money, and save most of it for later, in hindsight, whatever that means. My mother had a pretty simple strategy in life. Do what has to be done, no second guessing, no hesitation, just action. It's something that I can appreciate today much more than back in the days. Another thing that I can appreciate much more today than when I was young, is her gratefulness. Even today, my mother has the capability to look at small things with appreciation and a conscious sense of gratitude - the smile she gets from a cashier when paying her groceries or the helping hand from a neighbour; it all matters to her. There is pretty much nothing that she takes for granted.

Furthermore, my mother has always had an eye for beauty, which she most probably inherited from my grandpa, who was not only an accountant (yes, it looks like I also inherited something from him), but also a musician and a painter. In quiet moments, my mother would watch clouds passing by or follow a butterfly flying by from one blossom to the next. When I reminisce about my time at home, I always remember these moments. My father was not the talking type much, but he lived by example. I still remember when I was probably 19, and I brought my father to Rotterdam to take over a ship for the following six to eight months. He gave me a tour through the engine room, and what I saw was really impressive. The sheer size of the engine and all the things needed to keep the ship going allocated over a couple of floors were amazing.

Apart from that, it was an engine room, and the smell of oil and emissions filled the air. No matter where you put your hand, that space was full of dust, dirt, and grease. It was apparently a ship that had crossed the globe several times over already. When I left the ship, I waved at my father for the last time and passed the next months alone with my mother at home. But the day I picked him up again after around eight months turned out to be amazing for two major reasons.

First, I was seeing my dad again after all this time, knowing that he would stay with us for the next three to four months. Secondly, he gave me one more tour of the engine room, but this time it looked different. The engine room was freshly painted. It did not have an oil film on the handrail. It was so clean that you could safely eat from the floor. I still don't know how my dad managed that. You need to understand that, at that point in time, the shipping industry had gone through a massive change. The cost pressure had been high, and the nostalgic period was over. The ships no longer sailed under a German flag; instead, it was Panama, for example, where it was much cheaper to register a ship. The crew normally composed of people from the Philippines. Only the Captain, the Chief Officer, and the Chief of the Engine came from Germany. I need to add that my dad didn't have a talent for languages, so my question was; how on earth did he communicate with the crew to achieve the results that he did.

In hindsight, it is pretty clear to me now. He had simply lived by example. He had shown the crew what he wanted them to do. There was no task that he couldn't do himself. There was nothing that he was afraid to showcase so that other people could learn from it and thrive. Today, Robin Sharma would call him a leader without a title, if he had met him, and I am proud that I can call him my dad.

He showed me how to be honest to myself and do things right. If you make a decision to start a project, do it right from A to Z. If there is a lack of determination for you, it is better that you don't start anyway. Excellence meant a lot to my father, and on his way to perfection, he never stopped before he reached at least an excellent result. This could be a lesson for all of us; never stop until you have achieved the result that truly satisfies you. If you reach an excellent status, you need to have the courage to stop chasing perfection and let go. If perfection is still your ultimate goal, you will never achieve anything as perfection is an illusion. Trust yourself and stop when it is good enough. The rest will take care of itself.

I went to school, and I loved being involved in sports! However, the rest was just a necessary evil. At least I was clever enough to apply the rule that good horses are not jumping higher than necessary, which gave me ample time to spend doing all kinds of sporting activities. My path to success (I will come back to the definition of success a bit later) was paved right from the start – high school, military services, studying business administration (MBA), and then starting my career as a public accountant in a Big Four Audit firm. I passed the exam to become a Certified Public Accountant in New Hampshire/USA and continued to crunch numbers. It all went fine. I moved on to the headquarters of Deutsche Telekom in Bonn and later on was responding to a call from Luxembourg to start a career in financial services. In a nutshell, my professional career was on track.

And still, there was this feeling within me as if someone had put me on standby. It felt like being switched off— with the tiny but important difference that I could still hear, see, smell, and feel everything– unfortunately, without any chance to act or react. It felt like I was standing in front of traffic lights that were just showing amber light, waiting for green or red to appear any time soon, but it just didn't change.

I waited for as long as I could, but nothing happened. It is this situation of sitting in between two chairs, neither left nor right, neither yes nor no, no stop, and no go! What's left is the impression of uncertainty and confusion.

In September that year, my birthday came by. As a big surprise, my wife made me an unexpected gift. Apart from the fact that she had organized a great day for me including meeting with good friends over lunch in a fabulous restaurant and a visit to one of my favourite suit shops (yes, I am a little fashion victim), she had also arranged for a meeting with a personal coach a couple of days later.

Energized by that day, and with the outlook of meeting with a professional coach, I used the next couple of days to reflect a little on my own life and I tripped over a thought that hit me like a lightning bolt.

Why did I feel empty and not fulfilled despite the fact that I had done everything that society had asked me for to lead a successful life?

I just couldn't get the idea out of my mind that I had signed a contract right after I had joined the carousel of life. A contract that clearly defined all terms and conditions that made sure to enter the highway to success. Anything less was just unacceptable!

Rewind to where it began – it is September 17th 1968, and I just popped out of my mother's belly. So far, so good. I had nine months' time to get prepared for this moment. While my limbs were growing, and I was developing my senses, I could get a glimpse of what was going on out there. The more I could connect with the outer world, the more I was getting curious and keen to see what was waiting for me. In other words, I couldn't wait to get on stage and be the rock star of my life. So, the moment it happened, and I immediately got into the starting blocks waiting for the magic words: "On your marks, ready..."

Instead, I found myself sitting directly in front of a contract that was presented to me by society.

The contract read:

AGREEMENT FOR A SUCCESSFUL LIFE

THIS AGREEMENT is made and entered into this 17 day of September, 1968 by and between the SOCIETY, hereinafter referred to as "LEADER" and Dirk Sanden, hereinafter referred to as "FOLLOWER."

1. The parties agree that in case the follower applies all rules of professional success of the society listed in paragraph (2), the leader will deliver success as defined in paragraph (3).

2. The SOCIETAL RULES of professional success

a. Keep both feet on the ground, stay realistic, and don't dream.

b. Make sure to align with the rules and values of society.

c. Go to school, focus on maths and science, and get good A-level results. Study at a faculty with a high reputation.

d. Pass the exam to become an MBA or Ph.D. and add subject matter expertise to your curriculum on a regular basis.

e. Choose a reputable Big Four Audit firm or global law firm to start your career.

f. Get clarity on what the employment market is looking for and focus on the respective expertise.

g. Absorb as much information as possible to become a subject matter expert.

h. Play fair, but don't lose your professional focus.

i. Learn politics and play ball with your employer.

j. Learn the written and (especially) the unwritten rules of society and develop political acumen.

k. Don't mix your private life with your professional life.

3. PROFESSIONAL SUCCESS is defined as:

a. Financial security (ongoing salary payments & pension rights, health insurance, and car allowance).

b. A reputable social status.

c. A nice house, a big car, and a motorbike.

d. Vacation at exotic places at least two times per year.

Bremerhaven, September 17th, 1968

Dirk Sanden _ _ _The Society_ _

Signature	Signature
The Follower	The Leader

You're probably thinking right now: how on earth can you reduce your professional career to the above-listed terms and conditions? Especially as there is so much more to receive apart from material well-being. And I agree. Now!

However, back then, this was the contract, and I had signed it, just like many others on this planet.

Interestingly, almost 47 years later and drawing the balance, I realized that both parties had delivered. I applied the rules of society, the written ones, and also the unwritten ones that you cannot find in any official HR handbook.

As per the contract, society paid back by delivering monthly pay checks, bonus payments, pension schemes, and other financial goodies. In other words, no one was in breach, and still, it felt like having been tricked or at least having had overlooked parts of the small print. In hindsight, it is, of course, part of a never-ending learning process. Today, I feel much clearer on my expectations and the definition of success. Financial success is surely an important part of the game called life, but not the most important one. I equated success with achieving a certain amount of money and material wealth. Now, I define success much more broadly, simply as the achievements of MY goals, not someone else's – sounds pretty straight forward and actually it is. It's the moment you get clarity on what you really stand for, what you want in life, what really matters to you, and even more importantly, what your purpose in life is.

I learned that life is not supposed to be fair; it is supposed to be what I make out of it. So, now I am successful by setting clear intentions paired with a strong faith. I put necessary action and live my purpose supported by a set of inerrable basic values. The goals give me my destination. The action points define milestones. And my purpose, along with my core values and beliefs, give me orientation whenever I enter uncharted waters. By following this simple, but highly effective rule, I can live a life filled with purpose, deep satisfaction, and abundance. How this impacts life and how it changes the way of living and the worldview in general is the subject of this book. *Your Lighthouse Journey* offers a formula that can be applied by anyone who is looking for a meaningful, deeply satisfying life. So, go on, read, study, develop, and have fun while you are creating your very own Lighthouse Journey!

How to Read This Book?

I am neither a professor nor a scientist. This book is not written out of an ivory tower stuffed with lots of theories. Nevertheless, this book offers an idea of how to live your life based on fundamental principles that are already known for millennia. I put these principles and golden life rules in perspective and validate them on a daily basis to decide which one of them is the most useful for everyone depending on the situation or the challenge we face.

I keep this book very practical with lots of examples and techniques that can be applied to everyday life. One of my cornerstones in life is to keep things simple. This, together with the conviction that everybody on this planet has already everything at hand to lead a successful life, raises the following question:

"If it's true that most of our questions can be answered by applying common sense, what holds us back so persistently to turn these answers into common practice?"

This book gives an answer to this question. It encourages everyone to pause, reflect, and re-think how they've lived life thus far. It reminds people to step out of their comfort zones and break routines that have been established in the past and have never been questioned since then. This book suggests that you get rid of your blinkers and develop a 360-degree view of life. It asks you to get your nose off the canvas, step back, and see the bigger picture. It will teach you to focus your attention on the present moment. The days to live a life as part of the majority are counted, your life as a follower comes to an end – now, it's all about you and your authentic self. This book will show you the path to living the life of the minority; the life of a leader.

Last but not least, as I have already explained – I have a weakness for lighthouses. While reading through this book, chapter by chapter, we will build a new lighthouse (life), respectively, for you. It will culminate in erecting an all-new, rock-solid building that will stand for your fulfilled, joyful life, ready to be a beacon for others. That´s the ultimate goal in life. Once you succeed in living a life full of passion and joy, you need to be the guiding light for someone else.

I wish you a lot of fun while reading this book, to explore your best self, and start being the architect and keeper of your very own lighthouse.

Who Should Read This Book?

I would like to be clear with you right from the start. This book is not addressed to people who struggle with their lives, not getting anything done and blaming society for their unwillingness to take responsibility. I'm not saying that those people cannot learn by reading this book. They can actually learn a lot. But to be ready for the upcoming pages, you should have reached a certain level of openness and awareness that would have prevented you from being in this blaming game phase of your life in the first place.

So, if you still want to keep on reading, fair enough. But, please, let me give you a small yet important tip before we dive in. Stop being seated in the back seat of your car, complaining about the direction in which your car (life) is headed. Instead, put your buttocks in the driver seat, take the steering wheel, and make a conscious decision about where you're heading. But never forget: this comes at a cost.

You can't blame anyone anymore for what happens in your life. It's called responsibility. It is this incredible feeling that arises when your free will meets clarity about what really matters to you paired with intention and self-confidence.

This book is for people who are ready to leave the crowded highways of life and enter the small paths that are rarely used by the rest of society. Get ready to be part of the minority of people who live their lives on their own terms.

You've been warned, so proceed with caution!

For all other interested readers, the ones that have already succeeded in terms of understanding the success definition I have outlined above, I have great news. This is not the end of your journey; it is rather just the beginning.

The best is yet to come!

Contents

Page Left Blank Intentionally

Chapter 1
Awakening or Creating a Vision

"It is possible to experience an awakening in this life through realizing just how precious each moment, each mental process and each breath truly is."

-Christy Turlington

There is no doubt that human beings are the most intelligent creatures to have dominated the planet Earth. One thing that truly differentiates us from other living beings is our conscience and our ability to think and process information. Sure, there are studies that prove that animals also have thinking abilities, but they can't feel or process thoughts in the same way as us.

A daunting thing about the human mind that has baffled scientists over the years is the little voice in the back of our heads. This voice doesn't always translate into words for most of us. It stays in our heads, but it shapes ninety percent of our lives.

Strangely enough, some people actually love talking to themselves and may even have a name for this little voice in their heads. However, there's no need to worry for those who haven't named theirs as researchers have done it for them. The scientific name for this voice is 'inner speech.'

Every person is unique when it comes to their appearance, lifestyle, likes and dislikes, and several other things. Similarly, when it comes to inner speech, people have different perceptions of it as well. Some people describe it as their own voice while others differ themselves from it act more like an observer around it. Some people have multiple characters attached to their inner speech, and each of these characters has different viewpoints on every real-life situation.

I learned for myself that it helps to give your inner speech a name. It makes it more human, and whenever it pops up, you can consciously say hello and invite yourself to a little dialogue. Apart from that, it's pretty funny. My alter ego is currently called "Mr. Spoilsport." Depending on the situation, the name can change.

The inner speech (Mr. Spoilsport) is often ignored by many people as a mere thought that doesn't hold much importance in real life. However, there comes a time in life when these voices start making sense, especially when you have achieved all your basic goals and desires. This is a major sign that you have finally reached a stable level of maturity in your life, and you understand the fact that there is more to life than just getting your paychecks and enjoying barbeques on the weekends.

At this stage, the 'little' voices in your head begin getting louder, and you finally have to start taking them seriously. These voices give you ideas about the difference between the things that are right and wrong for you at the moment you are living them. You start identifying the difference between doing things right and doing the right thing.

This voice ends up shaping your future. This is basically the awakening of your mind and a major sign that you have finally started to connect to your inner wisdom.

When we are young, we have some basic objectives and aspirations that we want to achieve in our lives. Some people have dreams that seem unachievable to the extent that they become unfulfilled desires for them in life. Such dreams range from becoming film stars to billionaires.

As we grow older, such dreams dilute, and we go for more realistic goals such as owning a house, a nice car, and starting a family by the age of 35.

These 'attainable' dreams are relatively easier to accomplish, and once you acquire all of them, you are left with an emptiness inside you. That's when the voice in your head tells you that there is more to life than just achieving material targets. You can realize many of your dreams even if you stay in the same house and with the same car for a long while.

There is no particular age or stage in your life that activates the mature mode of the voices in your head. You can be awakened in your 20s or maybe in your late 40s as it was the case with me. It could be anything that triggers you to 'wake up' in your life and realize your true potential.

What is a Wake-up call?

If we look at the literal meaning of the wake-up call, it is something you normally say to a concierge at a hotel to wake you up at a certain time so that you are able to catch your flight. Obviously, we are not going to discuss *that* wake-up call in this book as it is based on the wake-up call of your life. The concierge, in this case, is your inner wisdom that finally crawls up through the copse of your mental forest.

A wake-up call, though, doesn't always come to you through the inner speech from your brain. It could be triggered through a real-life event that leaves an immense emotional impact on your personality and teaches you a lesson that stays with you forever.

For example, a person who drives recklessly often learns to slow down the hard way after they meet a horrific accident. After that, a sane person would drive with care for the rest of their life. Of course, it doesn't always have to be a tragic incident that wakes you up in your life. Sometimes, it can also be an opportunity that presents itself to you, and finally, you realize that you can make the most of it before everyone else and turn your life around for good. Or it can be, like it happened to me, simply a voice that is getting louder year by year until you can't ignore it any longer. One of the best examples to look at, in order to understand the wake-up call through opportunity, is the life story of Jeff Bezos, who is the current CEO of Amazon and also the richest man in the world at this moment.

Jeff Bezos was born in 1964 in Albuquerque, NM. He grew up as a nerdy kid who was always fascinated with computers and electronics. He pursued a degree in electrical engineering later, and immediately after graduation, he started working in some of the biggest firms on Wall Street, such as Bankers Trust, and FITEL.

He found success at D.E Shaw (an investment fund) and became the youngest vice president in the company's history in 1990. For many of us, Bezos was living his dream life, and there is no sane person who would walk away from this sort of career. However, Bezos was aware of his own potential and was only waiting for his wake-up call. That occurred in April 1994. Bezos was working on his computer one day and stumbled upon a study regarding this new thing called the 'internet.' Bezos found out that it has been growing at an alarming pace of almost 2300% per year. Bezos describes this moment as his "wake-up call." He says that he was astonished at the fact that if something was growing that quickly, it needed to be considered seriously.

After realizing the potential of the internet, Bezos did what most people would never think of doing in their lives. He quit his scintillating and high paying job in Wall Street and headed west to Seattle, Washington, to start his new company, which we all now know as Amazon.

Bezos started Amazon in July 1994, from the garage of a two-bedroom house that he had rented in Seattle with his wife at the time. He decided that the best way to make money online was to sell books because they were relatively much easier to ship.

The interesting thing is that some people laughed at Bezos at the time and said that his idea was crazy. People also questioned why anyone would buy books online when there were libraries and massive bookstores out there. They didn't know that Bezos would have the last laugh in this case. Amazon exploded in popularity throughout the 90s, and just before the turn of the millennium, Jeff Bezos became a billionaire for the first time in world history. The take away from the life story of Jeff Bezos is that you need to find your wake-up call and you don't really have to wait for it to come to you. You may not know it yet, but life gives you exactly what you desire. Many of you may disagree with me now, but when you reflect on your own life, you will realize that this is exactly how life has been with you. Simply put, the phenomenon of life giving you what you want is known as, 'the law of attraction.'

With this thought in his mind, Bezos was resonating positive energy out in the universe. He knew from the beginning that he had the potential to do something great but he still continued on living a regular life and working a job. It wasn't until that he was finally awakened by an opportunity that would turn his life around that he looked to open his own company. So, what is your (still) hidden potential?

The questions that might arise in your mind after reading the last passage is, "how can you achieve something by simply releasing positive energy? How do you even release positive energy?" To answer these questions, you need to understand the Law of Attraction a little bit better.

Law of Attraction

The law of attraction is one of the most fundamental and powerful laws of the universe. It is always in effect and moves just like gravity. To put it in simple words, the law of attraction states that whatever you put your focus on will be attracted to you. If you want money in life, keep your focus on making money, and you will get it. If you want to develop a trustworthy relationship, keep all your focus on emitting trust and love, and you will eventually receive it.

If you are constantly feeling enthusiastic, passionate, joyful, excited, and abundant, then you are sending out positive energy to the universe, and you can expect to receive a great amount of positivity back. It is like when you throw a stone in the middle of a pond. The ripples develop circularly, and where they hit an obstacle, little ripples are sent back.

Similarly, if you are constantly in a state of stressfulness, anger, sadness, resentfulness, and anxiety, then you are resonating negative energy. In this case, you will receive something negative back.

The universal law of attraction will always respond enthusiastically to both negative and positive energies that you emit. It is up to you to decide your fate.

The law of attraction will be thoroughly discussed in its entirety in later chapters of this book. For now, I'll let Albert Einstein speak. For him, the first and most basic question all people must answer for themselves is the following:

"Is the universe a friendly place or a hostile place?"

In other words, it is up to you how you perceive the world: either as a friendly, loving place or as a hostile one – up to you to decide. Or as Einstein continues:

"For if we decide that the universe is an unfriendly place, then we will use our technology, our scientific discoveries and our natural resources to achieve safety and power by creating bigger walls to keep out the unfriendliness and bigger weapons to destroy all that which is unfriendly and I believe that we are getting to a place where technology is

powerful enough that we may either completely isolate or destroy ourselves as well in this process.

If we decide that the universe is neither friendly nor unfriendly and that God is essentially 'playing dice with the universe.' then we are simply victims to the random toss of the dice and our lives have no real purpose or meaning.

But if we decide that the universe is a friendly place, then we will use our technology, our scientific discoveries and our natural resources to create tools and models for understanding that universe. Because power and safety will come through understanding its workings and its motives.

God does not play dice with the universe."

How to Answer Your Wake-up call?

As it was mentioned earlier in the chapter, every human being on earth is unique in their own way. Therefore, the chances of you receiving a wake-up call just like the one Jeff Bezos did are pretty slim. You will receive yours too but in your own peculiar way.

So, what to do then?

You have to look for the wake-up call yourself! Now, don't go looking for it with a magnifying glass! Jokes apart, take lessons from your life. Learn from everything that you can. There are so many things going around in our lives that can be used as a wake-up call. For example, if you are stuck in the loop of an extremely boring routine that makes you hate your job and pretty much everything that happens after the working hours, then you can use this as your wake-up call. Explore other talents and capabilities in your leisure time that you can use to break out of this chain.

Here are some of the wake-up calls that you definitely need to answer in your life:

There Might be No Tomorrow to Appreciate What You Got

"If a man has not discovered something that he will die for, he isn't fit to live."

-Martin Luther King Jr

As sad and depressing as this might sound, but all good things do come to an end, which includes our lives just as well as everything else around us. Therefore, you need to be grateful for whatever you have going in your life because there might not be another day. However, this definitely doesn't mean that you shouldn't struggle to make your tomorrow better than your today. You can simply use the inevitable end of your life as a wake-up call and consider the reality that you might not have much time left to make things right for yourself and also for the people that you love and care for.

I recently published a blog post titled, *"Of Horses and Men"* on my LinkedIn page that explains this point through a wonderful real-life experience that I went through personally. It goes something like this:

"I decided to spend one long, romantic weekend in Vienna with my lovely wife. During this wonderful time, we visited amazing buildings, locations, and sites. The thing that really stood out to us was the "Fiaker" which is a horse-drawn carriage.

If you have ever been to Vienna, then you would have definitely noticed these wonderful carriages being pulled by the majestic horses across the city streets. It is a sight to behold to see these beautiful creatures sprinting alongside people and traffic while tolerating typical city noises. They also somehow manage to keep a steady pace while being under the control of their watchful handlers. When we were observing the horses, we noticed that their eyes were shielded from both sides. The little eye shields, as we discovered during our travels, are known as "blinkers," and they are specifically designed to keep the horses from being distracted by their surroundings and keeping them a safe means of transport. If the horses could see all the traffic around them, they would definitely freak out! By using the blinkers, the horses are able to focus only on their own path and move in the direction that the handler intends to take them to.

The sole purpose of the blinkers was to limit the peripherals of the horses so they can only focus on the path ahead. The blinkers are also worn by horses that are used in parades and races so that they aren't distracted during important events and disrupt them. Basically, it is a method of restraining the vision of a horse, so that they can only be controlled by the handler or the rider.

Unlike humans, horses don't really seem to have any problem with their limited vision as they have no knowledge of what they can't see. Life, to them, is just a tunnel rather than an open field full of opportunities to explore anything they wanted to.

The question that might pop-up in your mind after reading the above passage is, *"What does this have to do with me?"*

Watching these horses move around had me thinking that despite having the freedom of choice, we human beings are also moving around with an imaginary set of blinkers.

- Aren't we wearing the same blinkers ourselves?
- Isn't our view limited to the only place that's ahead of us?
- Have we really lost the capability to look right or left

and to explore all the available opportunities in life?

- Lastly, have we only started wearing the blinkers recently or were we given blinkers at birth...?

Ever since we took our first breath on this planet, we have been trained, guided, and conditioned in such a way that we need to behave and act in certain ways: ways that are "acceptable" and appreciated by the society.

We are expected to lead a typical lifestyle that consists of passing school to get a decent job so we can buy a nice house and start a family and then waste time in IKEA stores looking for a perfect coffee table and lamps for our houses. We are expected to live our lives in a loop that comprises five working days a week, getting paid monthly, and earning a few days off annually to go away and relax a bit.

This basic structure of our lives has hypnotized our society into thinking that this is the only way to live, and everything around us shapes us to lead our lives in this way. Our parents, education systems, social lives, economic conformity, and creativity force us to lead this particular lifestyle. Some words from my beloved mother that happen to be my favorite:

"You can't do this, what would the neighbors think about us?"

This is probably one of the most used sentences in almost every society in the world. I'll give you another one:

"Stop dreaming, get both feet on the ground, start working, earn some money, and save it for later!"

It is sad but true that, for most of us, life is just a carousel of routines. If we look at it closely, every year of our life is exactly the same. The same old working routine, a few days off, paying the same mortgage. We are stuck in this never-ending loop, and the main reason for that is because we can't see anything else.

However, it didn't start this way. . .

Let's get back to the analogy of horses with the blinkers. However, this time let's go way back and think about how we were born. Each one of us was born without any blinkers tied to our heads, just like a wild and free horse. Just imagine a wild Mustang horse roaming around in the plains of North America. This wild horse has no blinkers on his head. As a consequence, it has a 360-degree view of the endless horizon.

I just want you to imagine the sense of freedom from the perspective of the wild Mustang. Under deep layers of societal rules and responsibilities, you will be able to feel this freedom inside of you.

What if I told you that you could get rid of all these layers? You can remove all these layers, just like peeling off the multiple layers of an onion. Step-by-step, you can remove these layers. Soon, you will be able to discover your authentic self. You will be able to see all the available options and opportunities for yourself that have always been here for you, but you were unable to see them because you had blinkers on.

A person who possesses an open mind and is curious about what the world has to offer will simply be energized by looking at all these "new" opportunities to live a life that is balanced and fulfilled in every way.

Learn to enjoy your life day-by-day, hour-by-hour, minute-by-minute...

And never forget that a wild Mustang is living inside of you.

Charlie Brown: "We only live once, Snoopy."

Snoopy: "Wrong! We only die once. We live every day!"

Never Pass On An Opportunity

"Opportunity does not knock, it presents itself when you beat down the door."

-Kyle Chandler

Keeping in mind the first reason that we all have limited time, not trying something out of the fear of failure, might turn out to be your biggest regret in life. Life will present you with amazing opportunities that you will only be able to see if you have been awakened. A huge lesson can be learned in this respect from the history of a company named 'Xerox,' which is a company still famous for producing reliable photocopy machines.

Xerox was founded in 1906 and pretty much ruled the first three quarters of the 20th century as the top photocopier in the world. It became so humongous that it pretty much monopolized the entire market share in its industry. After raking in an incredible amount of profits, it decided to lay the foundation of 'PARC.' an abbreviation for Palo Alto Research Center in 1970. It was a research and development company.

\- PARC was given a blank check from the mighty Xerox to recruit some of the best minds from all over the country, which it did. The company started producing different prototype devices. The most notable and famous invention to come out of PARC was the 'Xerox Alto,' which was the first-ever personal computer in history with a GUI (Graphical User Interface). This was a revolutionary invention that would, later on, change the course of history when it comes to the world of personal computing. However, Xerox executives failed to see any potential in the Alto and decided not to pursue its production and marketing for its eventual sales. That's because Xerox was too bloated from their never-ending success in the field of photocopiers.

So, what happens when you let an amazing opportunity like this go? The answer to that is that someone else picks it up.

In 1979, a young man named Steve Jobs (he founded this small company called Apple Computers) visited the PARC offices in Palo Alto, CA, to check out this revolutionary device that they had created. Jobs, who is regarded as one of the most visionary minds of the last century, was blown away after seeing the Xerox Alto up close. It was all he had imagined and dreamt of while developing the Apple I computer with his friend, Steve Wozniak. Jobs was astonished that Xerox showed no interest in developing this world-changing device, so he decided to capitalize on this idea and started developing the GUI for his computer based on the Alto. Apple would launch 'LISA' in 1983, and the world would be introduced to the first-ever 'all-in-one' personal computer with GUI.

Today, Apple Inc. is the largest tech company in the world by a significant margin. Xerox, on the other hand, is merely a shadow of what it used to be, simply because it decided to throw away a revolutionary idea. Of course, after giants like Apple, Microsoft, and IBM emerged as the leaders of the computer world, Xerox regretted it massively as photocopiers became less popular in the digital age that we are living in right now.

You must be ready to seize any opportunity that you deem right for yourself. Holding yourself back due to fear of failure or any other reason might result in life-long regret.

So, the next time when someone (maybe your boss) asks for a volunteer, you better take a step forward, a step towards the unknown, a step out of your comfort zone, a step towards where life unfolds.

Patience Is the Key

"Patience, persistence, and perspiration make an unbeatable combination for success."

-Napoleon Hill

After you have finally found your wake-up call, you don't have to just rush into things all at once. Sometimes, patience can be your key to success. For example, some people immediately quit their jobs after finding a brilliant business idea without any proper backup plan. This can be a huge gamble as there is no guarantee in life that things will always go your way. Therefore, keep your eyes on the prize while you work to achieve your goals slowly and gradually.

Some people take the advice of staying patient the wrong way and end up doing nothing at all to satisfy their inner voice along with their regular routine. As a result, they always feel a void in their lives that they can't seem to be able to fill up with anything. Patience can be a big challenge, especially when you are part of the millennial generation that is used to instant gratification. This generation quits jobs after a couple of months because they haven't made "an impact." Even in the digital world, life happens when we meet people and build deep, meaningful relationships.

Fundamental things that really matter in life like the love of life, job fulfillment, self-confidence, etc. need time to grow, like a seed put in the fertile ground that needs time to grow and care. As Simon Sinek puts it, these young people can only see the summit of Mount Everest, but they can't see the mountain itself. It is important to teach them how to build and use base camps to ultimately reach the peak.

No One is Perfect, Including You!
"Imperfection is beauty, madness is genius and it's better to be absolutely ridiculous than absolutely boring."

-Marilyn Monroe

Imperfections are what make us human beings. We are not programmed like robots to follow a certain track of instructions. We have the ability to make choices and follow our desires, which makes us adventurous, but sometimes it can be a bit distracting as well. Therefore, we end up making mistakes. However, we need to learn from these mistakes on our way because repeating the same mistake over and over again will get you nowhere in life. You can use your imperfections as a wake-up call and strive to improve them one-by-one.

It is your choice. You can call it a failure, or you can call it character building. Life throws challenges in our way to test our persistence and our commitment. Never forget that perfection is only a theoretical construct that doesn't really exist. So, the next time you're on your way to perfection, you simply stop at the level of excellence (or good enough) and let it go.

On my LinkedIn page, I published a blog post titled "*Life is like... Growing Tomatoes*", where I talk about how some projects actually seem to move slower, the harder you force them to move forward and speed up. In this, I analogize such a project with the act of growing vegetables in a garden:

"When you have a garden and you want to grow vegetables, you also have a project that you are passionate about. You also do everything that is necessary to make this project a success. You get clarity on what you want to grow; you prepare the soil in springtime, plant the seeds, and take care of the small, delicate sprouts. You constantly water it and make sure that the weed is not taking over, and by the end of the summer, you see the fruits growing until they are ready to be harvested.

My question to you is, why are we patient enough in the second example (growing vegetables) to wait until - somehow magically - the result turns up, but we are not as patient in the first example?

The answer seems logical and ridiculous at the same time. Of course, we all trust in nature when growing fruits. So, why don't we trust in something that is bigger and more powerful than us when working on specific projects or even creating our lives? Nature is always around us; it sets the pace for how our life unfolds and thinking that we can control everything is rather an indicator for our arrogance than a sign of wisdom. In that sense, trust is the answer to everything, no matter whether you grow tomatoes, prepare for a big business win, or develop deep relationships. So, next time, when you face this situation, stop pushing, believe in the ultimate success, and LET IT G(R)O(W)."

Doing the Right Things instead of Doing Things Right

"Do the right thing. It will gratify some people and astonish the rest."

-Mark Twain

It can be really confusing to understand the difference between doing the right thing and doing things right, but once you do get this, you become unbeatable. Doing things right simply means that you are following a set of instructions that has been developed by someone else or by yourself.

For example, if you are working in a company, you have to follow a certain set of rules in order to achieve a specific target. However, it doesn't necessarily mean that doing things right will always lead to success as you might be doing the wrong thing in the right way without realizing it. A great way to elaborate this point is by understanding the golden circle that was explained by Simon Sinek, a British-

American author, in his 2009 TEDx speech. Sinek simply drew three circles on a sheet on top of each other. He named the outermost circle as "What." the middle circle as "How" and the innermost circle as "Why." Sinek started explaining his golden circle through the example of Apple Inc. The world recognizes it as the most innovative technology company out there despite other companies making similar products. The main difference between Apple Inc. and its competitors is that Apple Inc. focuses on 'why' instead of 'how' and 'what.' Other companies waste precious time on 'how' and 'what.'

While all the other companies would simply market their products by telling everyone what they have created and how their products can help them on a day-to-day basis, Apple Inc. shares its belief with their target audience and markets its products by telling everyone that they believe in changing the world for good (The WHY).

For example, during the launch event of the Apple iPhone in 2007, the founder and CEO of the company, Steve Jobs, simply claimed that they have 'reinvented the phone.' However, touch screens were already available in the market even before the announcement of the launch of the iPhone.

Yet, most people remember them as revolutionary devices that changed the smartphone industry forever.

Why do you think that is? (We come back to the '*why*' again!)

That is because, unlike other companies, who marketed their products by simply explaining the '*how*'s and the '*what*'s, Apple Inc. explained '*why*' they had created a touch screen phone that was going to change the world. They believed in their goal and conveyed a clear-cut message to their target audience so that they can believe in their goal as well, which was to reinvent the phone and how the world looked at it. They wanted to make it more than just a means of communication.

Another great example that Sinek included in the explanation of his golden circle rule was about the first-ever flight by the Wright brothers. If you go and ask a 5th grader who were the first people to take flight in the world history, they will probably reply immediately that it was the Wright brothers. That's how famous these two brothers who repaired and sold bicycles for a living from Dayton, Ohio are.

However, if we take a deeper look into history, then we will find out that things weren't easy for the Wright brothers. The entire world had their hopes on someone else to take this giant leap for human civilization. A man named Samuel Pierpont Langley was assigned the task of researching and developing the first flying machine (an airplane) by the end of the 19th century by the U.S. government. He was also given a large budget and endless resources.

Using these resources, he gathered some of the most brilliant engineers from all over the country and got them all working on developing the first-ever successful aircraft. Langley's team successfully developed and flew some unmanned aircrafts with the help of catapults, during the next few years. However, they failed drastically while developing a manned aircraft.

Meanwhile, the Wright brothers (Wilbur and Orville) were enthusiastically working on their project without any kind of pool of resources helping them through it. They were exclusively driven by their unprecedented passion for being the first people to fly. After several failed attempts, the day eventually arrived. On the cold morning of December 17th, 1903, their model aircraft named 'Wright Flyer I' took its first-ever manned flight with Orville on-board. Wilbur ran alongside the wingtip to witness this historic event that would change the world forever. So, how were the Wright brothers able to defeat mighty Langley despite their shortcomings in almost all departments? The golden circle can give you a straight answer to that. That's because the Wright brothers set out to change the course of human history instead of earning fame and money, which was Langley's driving force.

They also believed in what they were doing, and they all gave their blood, sweat, and tears. The people who worked for Langley instead were only there because they were getting a fat paycheck. This is why almost no one remembers Samuel Pierpont Langley today, and almost everyone knows who the Wright brothers are. So, the next time you want to achieve something, start by asking yourself why you want to achieve it in the first place.

Doing the right thing is what all of us need to do in our lives, and it is only achievable once you have been awakened. An awakening will broaden your vision, and you will be able to see the outcome of the goal that you are working for clearly enough to decide whether or not it is the right thing to chase. Therefore, you need to assess your current life situation and opt to do the right thing instead of just doing things right. This may be the wake-up call you needed after all.

Wake-up calls are an important aspect of your life that you definitely need no matter what you do or where you go. However, a wake-up call without a proper vision in life can be useless. Therefore, every person should create a vision for their life and then use this wake-up call as a springboard to leap on the path of conquering their vision.

Creating a Vision

"Life is one big road with lots of signs. So, when you are riding through the ruts, don't complicate your mind. Flee from hate, mischief, and jealousy. Don't bury your thoughts, put your vision to reality. Wake up and live!"

-Bob Marley

It is quite astonishing that only a handful of people take their time to develop a proper vision for their lives. Success actually begins once you have a long-term vision set for yourself. Without a proper vision, your life will feel purposeless, and you will feel quite restricted in living it to the fullest. A vision is called vision because you can literally see it. The word derives from the Latin word Visio. So, if you want to create a strong vision, you need to have powerful pictures in your mind. Martin Luther King Jr. was a master when it comes to conveying messages based on a strong vision.

"I have a DREAM that one day... little black boys and little black girls will be able to join hands with little white boys and white girls as sisters and brothers!"

-Martin Luther King, Jr.

...By the way, he didn't state: "I have a PLAN..."

-Simon Sinek

Or as Patty McCord put it:

"People can't be what they can't see."

There are three major steps that every person needs to follow in order to create a perfect vision for their life:

- Learn from the Past
- Evaluate the Present
- Formulate a Vision for the Future

Let's explore these steps in detail.

Learn from the Past

"Some of the best lessons we ever learned are from past mistakes. The error of the past is the wisdom and success of the future."

-Dale Turner

Many influencers and life coaches often try to convey a message of leaving the past behind. It works to a certain extent, but the past is actually a part of our lives that whether we like it or not, it will forever stay in our memories. Our brains are not like computers that store good memories and get rid of the bad ones at our command. So, what to do with the mistakes and embarrassing moments from our pasts? We must learn from them!

Here, I would like to mention a few lines from another blog post of mine, titled *"Life is like . . . a backpacking trip."* that I published on LinkedIn as well. Go and read the full blog on LinkedIn when you can. I am sure it will give you a new perspective on life!

Here's how it goes...

"Have you ever, in your life, felt that you are carrying a huge weight on your shoulders all the time? Have you ever wondered if it is only you who is feeling this burden?

There are many people who experience this feeling of "traveling" all the time with a backpack hanging over their shoulders. Despite that, most people fail to realize that they are carrying this unnecessary load every single day of their lives while some of them are getting conscious about it and are thinking about what to do about it.

Which one of them are you?

The **first thing** you need to do is to take that "backpack" off your shoulders for a while and take a look inside. Determine what you have been carrying all this time. You might be able to find things that you will be happy to find out about.

The **first action** you need to take is NO action at all and simply accept everything that your backpack has to offer.

Every major change starts with accepting everything that the status quo has to offer. If you feel ashamed or concerned about accepting the rules from society and don't like what you see in the mirror, then it means you are raising awareness about what you really want.

The **second thing** you need to do is just be grateful for the fact that you are able to reach this level of consciousness. Appreciate and acknowledge the people who have helped you gain consciousness in the best way you can.

Your next step would require some courage from your side because opening the door to the next stage of your life is quite scary for some people. Why is that? That's because when they enter a new stage in life, they have to leave their comfort zone.

When you feel uncomfortable doing something, a little voice will ring out in your head and will start creating doubts and worries for you. You will end up feeling afraid of what's ahead of you. However, you need to convince yourself that you are doing the right thing and simply keep moving forward.

Moving forward, you will hear a motivating voice that will tell you that there is more out there that needs to be discovered. Listen to this voice carefully, take a deep breath, be courageous, and enter the carousel of life once more! This time, aim to live life on your own terms instead of following the routine that society has set for you.

By following this idea, you will be able to empty your heavy backpack step-by-step.

The past doesn't just provide a learning opportunity, but it also helps us close certain chapters of our lives and accomplish the things that we should have achieved years ago. Therefore, try to learn as much as you can from past mistakes, so you can avoid them in the future.

"There is no point studying the past unless it sheds some light on the present."

-James Hawes

Learning from past experience is important and is undoubtedly a cornerstone of life-long learning.

Here, I would like to briefly discuss another fundamental principle that we touched upon earlier at the beginning of the book: Letting things go. This principle comes in when you face challenging moments in your life that caused a hefty emotional reaction, e.g., someone didn't treat you nicely or even walked all over you. The body, and respectively the subconscious mind, is storing those events in the form of an emotion that will hit the surface every time your mind creates thoughts about this event. This thought-emotion loop prevents you from moving on. Instead of allowing your body to take over and block you from focusing on the present time, you should take control. It doesn't need much from your side, just a bit of self-compassion and forgiveness. You didn't do anything wrong; it was just another opportunity to build your character. You need to let it go!

I would like to share a story with you that explains it perfectly.

There were once two monks on a pilgrimage. They were walking already over hours practicing noble silence when they reached a little village. It was raining and next to the road there was a young woman standing in a beautiful kimono. She was reluctant to cross the muddy road as she was afraid to soil her clothes.

The old monk took the lady and carried her over the muddy street and put her down on the other side of the road. The monks continued their journey, and after around five hours, when they almost reached the next village, the young monk broke the silence and said: "You know, it was not right what you have done. Monks are not allowed to touch women." And the old monk answered: "Are you still carrying the young woman? I put her down already hours ago."

Let it go!

Evaluate the Present

"Planning is bringing the future into the present so that you can do something about it now."

-Alan Lakein

After reviewing the past, you need to assess your current situation. The evaluation of the present should include all the critical elements of your life, such as work, family, finances, your physical health, where you stand emotionally, your personal development and your relationships with other people in your life.

Dr. Dispenza can put this into perspective for you through his blog, *'Making the Present the Present.'*

"Life moves pretty fast. If you don't stop and look around once in a while, you could miss it."

-Ferris Bueller

Ferris Bueller spoke this famous quote in 1986 when things weren't as complicated as they are now in today's modern, fast-paced world. Today, we are constantly moving from one thing to another. Before we can take a break, something new comes around the corner immediately. In this panicky scenario of a world, are we missing out on our lives, which is an ever-present thing in the world?

It is funny that we tend to miss out on our lives because we stay oblivious to the present moment. We often miss the present moment because we are only focusing on random programs such as, "I have to go get groceries, I have to wash my car, and I have to take care of something…"

The importance of the present moment should never be underestimated as it is our doorway to the future. The present moment also happens to be a place from where we send out to and receive from creation. We can also harness awareness and focus from the present moment in order to create and later receive creation. Why? Simply because energy flows where attention goes! So, you better pay attention to what you want to focus your thoughts on.

We are incapable of running a program while living in the present moment, which is why Dr. Dispenza has created some exercises for you that you should try out. It is up to you to either choose from these exercises or create your own. You need to start from smaller exercises and then gradually move on to the bigger ones.

Here are some of the exercises to break daily routines and get you closer to the present time:

- Almost all of us have some kind of daily commute. On this commute, simply try observing a tree throughout the entire season. It doesn't necessarily have to be a tree as it can be a small plant or a stray kitten that you daily see in your street. Basically, you can observe any living being that is growing and evolving through time.

- Pick a great spot with natural surroundings such as a garden, park, or woods. Stop at this spot for three to five minutes, close your eyes, and listen to all the sounds in the surroundings. Follow the sounds consciously.

- Pick a significant moment or event in your life that always reminds you to open your heart whenever you look at it.

- Download an app on your phone that reminds you

daily to live out your present moments to the fullest. The app, 'Chill' is a great option for it, give it a go, and you will be able to experience the change automatically.

- Look up at the sky during the night time, or
- Try to clean your teeth with the left hand (in case you are a right-hander) or vice versa

Last but not least, if you still have difficulties getting into the present time, stop talking, and instead, show interest in the people that are surrounding you. When you start asking questions, you are immediately in the present time and build rapport at the same time. And there is another positive side-effect:

"When you talk, you can only speak about something that you already know. When you start listening, there is a good chance to learn something new."

-Sadhguru

We can benefit a lot from investing our time in the present moment in this incredibly fast-paced technological world. That's because it is the present moment where the moments of awe and wonder tend to intersect with our spiritual and human experience. This is that time when life actually speaks to us. You should keep your vision in your mind while you assess your present situation of life. Think about how all of these things will look like in the vision that you have imagined for your life.

Formulate a Vision

"Vision without action is merely a dream. Action without vision just passes the time. Vision with action can change the world."

- Joel A. Barker

After reflecting on the past and assessing your current situation, you need to use them as a foundation to develop your vision. You need to create a long-term vision for where you want to see yourself after a few decades. After creating a long-term vision, you should be able to answer the following questions about yourself:

- Why do I have my two feet on the ground?
- What kind of person am I striving to become?
- What do I want to create?

- What am I working for?
- Who am I doing it for?
- What is the definition of a perfect day?
- What should my finances look like after 1, 3, and 5 years?
- What kind of legacy do I want to leave behind?

If you are able to answer all of the questions mentioned above, then it means that you have successfully developed a vision, and you need to start working to achieve it.

A major part of creating a vision includes considering the legacy that you are going to leave behind. If you want to live a purposeful life that leaves an impact on this world, then you also need to develop a vision for the time after you are gone. Therefore, you should also be able to answer the question, 'what will people think or say about you at your funeral?'

We are all walking to an inevitable end of our lives, which can be sad and depressing to think about. Who would want to leave behind such a beautiful life?

However, none of us can control death.

Preparing for your death should also be a part of your long-term vision instead of taking it as a negative point in your life. I would like to give a very practical recommendation before leaving this chapter. As I said before, vision means you make your goals visible. You produce pictures in your mind that will guide you towards the desired outcomes.

I understand that not everyone has the creativity to visualize a target. In addition, sometimes we can't even step out of our pre-conditioned way of thinking. No one taught us so far to dream our wildest dreams. If you belong to this group of people, I have a brilliant solution for you; book a vision board session with a local consultant or coach. A vision board is a collection of your innermost desires put as pictures on a piece of paper.

During the session, you have the chance to flip through tons of magazines and search for YOUR pictures. Interestingly, somehow (remember the law of attraction), you will attract the right magazines with the right pictures. Sometimes you are surprised about the outcome as you will find pictures that simply resonate with you and show things that you didn't dare to think of so far. In other words, it tricks your brain (your rational mind) and let the heart take over.

Once you have that vision board ready, put it in a frame and hang it where you can see it every day.

If you still need another motivation to kick-start your new life, how about this analogy. There was once a man lying on his death bed surrounded by ghosts. Each of the ghosts represented one single, un-explored (and hence wasted) talent of the man. They looked at him, and very sadly, just before he passed away, they explained that they all have to die together with him, without any chance left to thrive. Here is my question: How many ghosts will surround you when you will do your last breath?

The sooner we wake up and realize our true potential, the sooner we will be able to turn our life around and create a perfect future for us. This is the foremost step in beginning to rebuild your life. By the end of this book, I will make sure that you will have all the steps necessary for rebuilding your life the way you want to!

We have kicked off our journey towards joy and abundance by setting the scene here. We got a glimpse of how we can make the most of our wake-up call and read about inspiring stories of people in the society that accelerated their lives dramatically. In the next chapter, let's discuss some fundamental assumptions for living a good life. We need to agree on some ideas that we can use to give us direction for the following chapters and the journey that we are on now.

Chapter 2
Preconditions for an
Accelerated Life

"Your assumptions are your windows on the world. Scrub them off every once in a while, or the light won't come in."

-Isaac Asimov

Making assumptions is probably one of the easiest things that you can do in life. All you need to do is possess incomplete knowledge about any situation along with the unwillingness to ask any questions about that information, and then voila, you can draw your own conclusion by filling in the blanks.

You tend to fill these blanks with your own interpretation of whatever you hear, see or understand yourself. Most of the time, these interpretations are drawn from past experiences and also from what you have heard from others. With all the information you have at this point, you try to connect the dots that aren't actually there. You also can't help yourself from connecting these dots because you do not have any relevant information. Therefore, instead of trying to make sense of the actual situation, you tend to jump to the conclusion. This sounds as if it is a conscious decision, but it´s not. The subconscious mind is doing this naturally, simply to protect us from doing things that could put our lives in danger.

The question arises; who should run the show? The subconscious mind or the conscious mind? The answer is as usual: somewhere in the middle. It depends on the situation. Let´s say it is 50.000 BC and you are strolling through the plains. You hear a noise behind a bush, and your subconscious mind immediately fills the information gap with some assumptions that it could be a sabre-toothed tiger waiting for his lunch.

The immediate reaction of the body is to create a stressful situation (fight or flight mode) to be prepared for the worst, and then you flee as fast as you can. The result is that you still don´t know whether your reaction was justified, but you are still alive. Pretty good life insurance, right? Let´s compare it with the scenario when the conscious mind takes over. You hear the noise behind the bush, and your scientific mind tries to close the information gap by investigating. The thought would be: "Interesting sound, what could it be, let's find this out!" This could lead to a situation that you might find your lunch in the form of a rabbit, or it might end in a situation that there is actually a predator waiting for you, and the following thought is your last: "Interesting. Now, I know how a sabre-toothed tiger sounds like. So, I am smarter now; but dead!"

The art of dealing with assumptions is to find the middle ground. We need to better understand in which situation we let the autopilot work, e.g. to save energy when we actively need to make assumptions consciously and what influence do our emotions have. Let's dive into it.

How Do Assumptions Develop?

Assumptions have manifold consequences, especially when dealing with rational matters. The question that comes to mind at this point is that what happens when emotions come into play?

The answer is that all hell breaks loose. Emotions often contain many sensitive areas. Particularly, these are the areas where you got hurt in the past. The pain you felt back then comes back due to emotions. Even if your current situation is completely different from the past one, emotions can still trigger the same pain.

Let's have a closer look at the interaction of assumptions and emotions.

Assumptions and Emotions

Due to all the energy (positive and negative) radiated by assumptions along with the triggering of the respective emotional reactions, we should be mindful of the powerful impact that assumptions can have on our life. Here are some reasons why we should be conscious of what false assumptions can trigger:

- **They are the easy way out:** The path that comprises of least resistance is also the path of least resistance.

- **They prevent you from taking responsibility for your own life:** Using assumptions, you tend to hide behind your own version of the story. This means that you refuse to own your part in the true story. You rather blame others for your own mistakes and misfortune.

- **You are stuck in the past:** Since assumptions mostly rely on information from the past to connect the dots, it causes you to retreat back in time, especially to the painful past of your life.

- **The lazy behavior:** Instead of inquiring about the truth, you tend to draw conclusions on your own.

- **The negative mindset:** Most of the assumptions are the derivations of old and painful information from your past. This develops into a negative mindset, and everything in and around the world seems miserable to you.

- **You develop toxic behavior:** In order to protect yourself from getting hurt, you use your own assumptions to lash out on others. This is bad for your relationships with other people.

- **They are a bad habit:** The more assumptions you make and the more consistently you apply them, the easier it gets to turn them into a habit.

- **They are almost always wrong:** Nearly all of the assumptions that you are going to make will be wrong. However, there are some of them that can actually be right (will be discussed later on in the chapter).

The above examples might resonate with you. Most probably, they will as it is human to go the easy way, to find excuses, and to blame society for things that go sideways in our life. Here is the learning. Don't beat yourself up for having these thoughts and making certain assumptions that might not serve you best right now. Instead, congratulate yourself for understanding the background of these emotions and acknowledge that they are a normal part of you. The next step is accepting them and turn them in something positive. Let's look into techniques on how to do this.

One of the best ways to avoid making destructive assumptions is by asking questions. You need to question everything, even if the truth might seem a bit painful to you. A painful truth will be much better than a sugarcoated assumption.

How to Stop Making Destructive Assumptions

Negative assumptions can have a hefty toll on your health and relationship. That sad thing is that most of us do it in our lives. For example, if a friend forgets to call you when he/she is visiting your town, and you find it out through their social media, you automatically assume that they don't value you anymore. You draw a conclusion in your mind and develop a grudge for something that you are not even completely aware of.

"While you judge me by my outward appearance, I am silently doing the same to you, even though there's a ninety-percent chance that in both cases, our assumptions are wrong."

-Richelle E. Goodrich

Assumptions are one of the basic functions of our brains. Our brains have evolved over time to keep us safe in this chaotic and ever-changing world. This has provided human beings with an incredible ability to take pieces of information and then fill in the blanks to draw the conclusion. Sometimes, the assumption can be beneficial for us, while at other times, it can have negative consequences.

Human beings are pretty resourceful and resilient species. This system of making assumptions has evolved in a specific context that is different from our everyday environment. Therefore, we now have the opportunity to continue the evolution.

Below are some of the ways that can help you train your brain to stop making negative assumptions.

Stop Judgement

Notice everything happening around you without being judgmental about anything. This practice is pretty effective and transformational in many ways. Even in your thoughts, you should notice everything without judging anything.

"If you judge people, you have no time to love them."

-Mother Teresa

Draw Multiple Conclusions

All the negative assumptions that overwhelm your mind are often based on the negative beliefs that you hold about yourself. Another trickery of the human mind is that the more you think about something, the more real it seems. For example, if a friend doesn't invite you to a party, you begin to think that they are avoiding you or don't value your company anymore. This negative belief continues to circle your mind, and you start believing in it as gospel. The reality might be that they simply forgot about inviting you or the party was for their other social circle, consisting of people that you don't know at all.

One way to avoid it is by drawing multiple conclusions. Thinking about other possibilities can weaken the negative belief, and it also trains your mind to stop settling on one conclusion only.

Investigate Your Worst-case Scenario

Let's continue the example that we used in the previous point about not getting invited to a party. The worst-case scenario that comes in your mind regarding the event is that people at the event didn't want you there. Somehow, you find out that it was actually true, and in reality, one particular didn't want you there.

Before you start wondering what everyone at the event thinks about you and start feeling insecure, you need to make a choice. Many people start feeling powerless in the worst-case scenario, which makes them feel like everything is out of their control. They start looking for answers and resolutions to make them feel better. You need to understand the fact that you are never powerless, even during your worst-case scenario.

Considering the same example of not being invited to a party, here are a couple of choices you have:

a. **Spiral Down Negatively:** You start thinking that if one person from the party (who prevented your invitation) doesn't like you, then all of the people that came to the party don't like you. You keep on thinking about how bad you are, and negativity keeps on spreading across your mind.

b. **Accept the Reality:** You can also accept the reality that all the people in the event might really not like you. You can ask yourself questions that did you really need to hang around people who don't value you? Did you really need to go to that party anyway? You could have utilized that time doing something productive or spent it with people that actually respect and value you.

Value Your Time

One of the major side effects of making assumptions is impatience. Since our brain provides answers pretty quickly during the process of making an assumption, we develop a habit of becoming impatient. One of the prime examples of impatience in today's world is texting and posting.

When you text with other people, you expect immediate replies from their side, especially if they are reading your messages. If they delay reply by even a few minutes, negative thoughts start developing in your mind. The best way to get rid of this impatience is to go do something else instead. The more you wait for a response to your message, the more assumptions your mind is going to churn out. Your time is limited, and you should utilize it in doing some other important instead of anxiously waiting and wondering what the reply will be or why aren't they replying immediately.

Assumptions can have negative effects, but it doesn't necessarily mean that they cannot be turned into positive outcomes, because they can.

When it comes to building your life back up, you want to define a couple of conscious, well thought through preconditions. One of them is the principle of free will.

Free Will

"Life is like a game of cards. The hand you are dealt is determinism; the way you play it is free will."

-*Jawaharlal Nehru*

Free will is basically just the ability to make certain choices in life. It is also related to the concepts of praise, responsibility, sin, and guilt that may apply to the actions that are chosen freely. It is also linked with the concepts of persuasion, prohibition, advice, and deliberation.

Free will is one of the most debated topics in the world of philosophy. There are two polar opposite sides when it comes to this debate. One side believes that human beings are free to do whatever they want in life, and they have complete control over their destiny. These are the people who believe in the existence of free will without any kind of boundaries or restraints.

The other side believes in determinism, which means that they believe in fate, and everything a person does in their life is already determined by past events in their lives. This is a bold claim, but it actually makes sense to some extent if we dig a bit deeper into it.

One of the greatest stories that explain determinism in a wonderful way is that of Oedipus.

Oedipus was a mythical Greek king of Thebes. He is most famously known for his incredible story that began when he was born. He was the son of Lauis and Jocasta, the king and queen of Thebes. The Oracle prophesied that any son born to Lauis would grow to murder him and then marry his own mother. Lauis believed in the prophecy, and after his son was born, he carried him out to the middle of the forest and left him there. The baby Oedipus was then found by a couple who took him and raised him as their own son. As he grew up, he learned about the prophecy and decided to leave his home to avoid it. However, he was unaware of the fact that the people who raised him weren't his real parents.

During his journey, Oedipus would kill a stranger and then marry his widow. The stranger he would kill would turn out to be his biological father; and his widow, whom he later married, was his actual mother — hence fulfilling the prophecy by doing what he was always afraid to do.

Of course, the story of Oedipus is actually a myth, but it doesn't mean that we can disregard determinism completely and automatically start believing in free will. What we really need to do is find a middle ground.

Each and every one of us has different needs in this area, which depends on the contrasting levels of these two psychologies, defeatism, and aspiration.

People who have reached high levels of defeatism often declare that they are not responsible for the things happening in their life anymore. They start blaming others, including their parents, the school system, the media, their bosses, and many others for their personal failures in life. In reality, however, this is nothing but just self-deceit and radical under-achievement driven by (in most cases, unconscious) limiting self-talk.

On the other side of the spectrum, some people reach incredibly high levels of aspirations on the basis of exaggerated notions of free will. These people firmly start believing that everything in their life can be changed when and how they want. They declare that everything in this world is achievable through an exercise of the will. However, when things start going south for these people (which they always do in life because it is full of ups and downs), they spiral down towards rage and bitterness.

At the end of the day, it gets down to your individual choices, whether you should have faith in free will or determinism. You should ask yourself how much suffering in your life can be traced back to ruthless aspiration and how much to the defeatist attitude. Some people need the mellow acceptance of determinism in their life while some need to believe in the wonders and possibilities of free will. One of the oldest debates in the world of philosophy has a definite answer, but it is more on the personal side of human beings rather than general.

One of the wisest ways to navigate between determinism and free will was laid out by the philosophers of ancient Rome. They belonged to the Stoic school. The Stoics believed that human beings are always hovering between the states of determinism and free will.

"You can choose a ready guide in some celestial voice/if you choose not to decide, you still have made a choice . . . I will choose a path that's clear - / I will choose free will.

-Rush (band) from their song "Free Will."

Drawing the balance now for my life and analyzing what drove my life so far, I can conclude that the beauty of free will is probably one of the most underestimated life concepts. How do you want to live your life? As a slave or as a master? Well, I prefer to live life as a master, meaning on my terms, and the principle of free will guarantee that I am the master of my thoughts. No one can tell me what I have to think. Let's digest that. We need to regularly remind ourselves of the importance of that sentence because it means we can sit in the driver seat of our lives (if we wish). In other words, it is a conscious decision to either think that life sucks or to think life is beautiful, full of fun, and opportunities. The difference between both situations is just one little thought, and we are fully responsible for what thoughts we let pass through our brains.

Isn't it interesting that we have the full power already inside of us to decide which way to go/think? What makes this principle so powerful is that we always have the choice to focus our attention on what really matters to us. As a consequence, we all have to ask one question. Do we want to live our lives on the back seat of the car or on the driver seat? Never forget that everything starts with a thought.

Everything in this life was created twice, first in someone's mind and then in reality, as Robin Sharma once concluded wisely. I concluded for myself that I want to have the steering wheel in my hand and drive my life the way I want. Does this come as a cost? Sure! I can't blame anyone for what happens in my life anymore. How cool is that? I love being responsible for myself and my life. If this is the cost of living a free life, bring it on, I'm ready to pay!

If you now sum the story up, you need to admit that there is no such thing as coincidence, because as Rene Egli in his book "The LOLA Principle" explained, it would be simply against the idea of the free will. So, never forget that the way you think impacts the way you feel and the way you feel has a direct impact on the way you act. In a rigid and destructive way, if we think negative thoughts. And in a constructive, fulfilling way, if we think positive thoughts. What a wonderful power that was given to us!

Balance between Body, Mind, Soul & Energy

In order to be successful in life, the connection between your mind, body, soul, and energy is undeniably important. However, in today's world, we seem to ignore this basic connection and rather focus on physical wellness factors such as healthy eating, working out to create an overall attractive appearance. Although physical wellness is important as well, it only fulfills part of the purpose if you ignore the mental and spiritual wellness along with it. One of the guiding principles of mind-body-energy medicine is the interconnection of all the things, including the environment that we reside in. Every one of us is an inseparable part of a never-ending field of intelligence or energy, and with every breath, we are exchanging millions of atoms with the universe. Let me share a short story about energy and the fact that everything (including a stone, a human being, and this thought that I just put here on paper) are made of energy, or atoms, which are composed of by the core and a certain number of electrons.

Interestingly, these components are only a tiny part of an atom. In fact, the space in between these particles represents around 99.99% of an atom. Assuming this vacuum is made of energy, vibrating with a certain frequency, we can conclude that everything on this planet is made essentially of energy. As energy has no boundaries and is communicating through vibrations (different frequencies/energy levels), everything is linked with everything else.

Consequently, we need to be careful with what we think (remember: a thought is also energy) as I can communicate with my environment non-verbally by the way I am thinking about it. If this reminds you now of what we have learned about the law of attraction at the beginning of this book, you got it! By purely thinking about my life and the people in my life, I am sending energy waves towards my environment in particular, and the universe as a whole. Since everything is linked, my energy will be reflected by the universe. Bad thoughts/energy will be reflected in the same way as the good, productive thoughts will be reflected – the law of attraction doesn't know the difference between good and bad thoughts. It simply sends you back what you have sent out. This is what I call unconditional fairness without any judgment. Again, it leaves full responsibility with the individual that creates the thoughts.

Back to the principle of free will, as stated above. Knowing the theory now, what kind of energy do you want to emit? Rhetorical question, isn't it? In other words, be very careful and make a mindful choice when thinking! We will come back to the importance of understanding the concept of energy in the next chapter.

From this amazing perspective, health isn't just the absence of the disease or symptoms; instead, it is an optimal state of wellbeing and wholeness. You are considered healthy if you are able to digest everything that you take in. This includes the food you eat, your job, relationships, and all other life experiences. It also means which thoughts you create depending on what life throws at you. Remember what we read in the previous chapter about the interconnection of assumptions and emotions. The way you think defines the way you feel.

In contrast, illness develops whenever there is a disruption in the flow of information and energy in your body and mind.

In order to create a perfect energy balance between your mind, body, and soul, I recommend to incorporate the following activities in your life:

Meditate

One of the best ways to get rid of stress from your life is meditation. You should take a few minutes out of your life daily to cut yourself off from the hassles of the world and sit in complete silence. Make sure to turn off your technology gadgets to avoid any distractions. Phones, tablets, and computers often drain energy and, as a result, increase the overall stress level. You need to let your mind be awake, observant, and alert while maintaining inner calm. If you fail to keep calm at the beginning, then your mind will likely wander off to work and induce stressful thoughts. In this situation, you must refrain from panicking and blaming yourself as it will do nothing but further boost the stress levels. Instead, focus again on your breath. Breathe in and out and observe how your body is behaving while inhaling and exhaling. What you need to do is observe your progress and see how you are able to improve meditation practices over time and pat yourself on the back for any improvement.

Never expect that you will get it right from the get-go. Many people struggle a lot when they start to practice meditation. That's because their minds aren't wired to stay calm due to incredibly dynamic and busy routines. It is a gradual process that requires practice and most importantly, patience.

Sadhguru gives the following advice, in case you really struggle with disconnecting from your daily treadmill. Sit in front of a water-tab, open it so that there are between 5 and 10 drops falling per minute. Watch the drops falling and observe how the drops are formed, released, and fall into the sink. Do this for around 20 minutes to calm your mind. Meditation is really important for all health aspects of life, especially for spiritual growth. You develop a relaxing attitude towards life if you practice meditation daily. It also helps you to align the wavelength of your energy with your inner wisdom and the universal energy that surrounds you.

Eat Healthy

The phrase 'you are what you eat' is literally true. This is one of the main reasons why many people emphasize the importance of clean eating a lot. Cutting out eating too much unhealthy food from your diet is known for contributing positivity in you. Of course, that means replacing it with a healthy diet such as organic fruits, vegetables, and lean meats. A healthy diet can also make you feel better about yourself, but it is alright to sometimes indulge in foods that you like regardless of whether they are healthy or unhealthy just to satisfy your cravings. Don't punish yourself for losing your grip on discipline once in a while – nobody is perfect!

One of the best ways to determine a balanced diet is to understand the tastes of the food. You need to make sure to include six basic tastes in each meal. These tastes comprise of sweet, sour, salty, bitter, pungent and astringent. A typical (unhealthy) American diet only consists of sweet, salty, and sour (common flavors of a hamburger) tastes. Although we do need to include these tastes, they are also known for lowering the metabolism if consumed in excess. The other tastes (bitter, pungent, and astringent) have an anti-inflammatory effect on the body, and they also boost metabolism. These tastes are commonly found in foods like ginger, pepper, radishes, spinach, tea, mushrooms, lettuce, lentils, and many others. You also need to avoid canned or processed foods and instead opt for fresh ones. These foods weaken your health and accelerate aging.

Never forget that food is the bricks that you need to build a strong, long-lasting house. Everything you have eaten so far in your life was transformed into what is now your body. Hence, doesn't it make sense to only use good, robust bricks to build a house that is worth to be called "my body"? Maybe we should change the expression "my home is my castle" to "my body is my temple." You would always respect the sacred place of a temple, wouldn't you? So why not doing the same with your body?

Exercise

Exercising daily does not only improve your physical well-being, but it also helps in enhancing your mental and emotional well-being. When you exercise, your body releases the 'feel-good' chemicals, which are dopamine, adrenaline, endorphins, and serotonin. These chemicals improve your mood and make you feel better and happier. In addition, exercise also enhances your cognitive skills and enables you to think better. In addition, it is a great stress reliever. Exercising is also known for keeping your body young and energetic. It also keeps the mind vital and promotes emotional well-being.

However, one of the mistakes that many beginners tend to make is they start with full throttle and then burn out quickly. This is not only the wrong way to do it, but it can also cause injury. Therefore, the best way to start exercising is slowly and gradually. Start by once a week with light exercise, and then start adding days and workouts as you develop muscles and stamina.

Reconnect to Nature

It is crucial for a balanced life to spend time in nature on a regular basis. Why is this so? Think about what the basis for our lives is and where it all began. Everything that you need to live a healthy life, you can find in nature. A lot of clean air and water. Guess where all the fruits and vegetables are coming from? Correct, they don't grow in your office – at least not yet. Apart from that, you might have felt it yourself while walking through a forest: the energy level in nature is much higher than in the city. This is simply because nature is the original source of energy, not the artificial environment of an office or a gym. When you have the choice to plug into the original energy source versus an artificially created one, what would you choose? We simply spend too much time in well-insulated environments that make it impossible to stay tuned with nature. By the way, when did you last walk through a rain shower in a park, listening to the falling rain and breathing in the fresh air?

Restful Sleep

Restful sleep is one of the most important activities that you should incorporate in your life in order to achieve success. People who don't get proper sleep tend to more tired and stressed all the time. This stress interferes with their daily life, and they end up making costly mistakes at work/school. Sleep is similar to a healing process as your brain consolidates the information it has received during the day and improves the memory as a result. This process happens during the rapid-eye-movement phase of your sleep. It is only after getting sufficient rest, due to sleep, that your body is able to take on the challenges of the next day.

People often fail to understand the importance of sleep and use it as a pool of hours that they can take off in order to squeeze in some more work. However, not getting enough sleep will actually deteriorate your performance at work, and it may take you longer to accomplish a task that could have been done in much less time.

Do Some Creative Activities

In today's hectic world, most of the people have burdened their lives with the stress that eventually accumulates all the pressure inside the body. You need to release this pent up pressure in order to feel calm and relaxed. One of the best ways to release the pressure is by finding some kind of creative activity that you are good at or just love doing. Some people tend to enjoy painting while some prefer writing. Whichever activity you choose, make sure to dedicate some time to it because it is necessary to release all the pressure from your body to avoid burning out. All of the five activities mentioned here are incredibly effective in maintaining the balance between mind, body, and soul. They have been proven by the people who have to practice them daily, and they have reported the benefits from the results as well.

Yoga

Last but not least, Yoga is an amazing mix between all of the above-mentioned ingredients of a well-lived life. Yoga is not only a physical exercise; it is an attitude. According to Sadhguru, *"Yoga is not an exercise form as is commonly misunderstood today. Yoga literally means union. Modern science proves that the whole existence is just one energy — but you are not experiencing it that way. If you can break this illusion that you are separate, and experience the oneness of existence, that is yoga."*

"Never allow your mind to wander untamed like a wild animal that exists on the basis of survival of the fittest. Tame your mind with consistent focus on your goals and desires."

-Stephen Richards

Or simply put: Be careful what you wish for!

As a side remark, all of the above-mentioned proposals can be enjoyed as a single experience or as a combined pleasure. For me, exercising in nature, for example, is like meditation. It takes around half an hour before my mind is cleared and all open issues are stored in the boxes of my brain where they belong. Just right after this phase of purification, my mind gets creative. Once back home, I have new innovative ideas or new projects (e.g. this book). I feel physically exhausted but mentally awake; my lungs are boosted with oxygen, and there is no sign of stress anymore!

The Link between Energy and Everything

"What we think, we become."

-Buddha

After focusing on the importance of balancing your mind, body, and soul, the next essential factor that requires your attention is the understanding of 'energy.' When it comes to energy, almost all of us have a similar understanding of this term, which is loosely based on what we were taught in school. Energy is just the capacity to do work, and it exists in many forms. We are constantly surrounded by energy at all times. Even light that helps us see is a form of energy. However, what we failed to learn back then is that everything is energy, even including human beings, and there's even a scientific explanation to this fact as well.

If we look at history, humans have believed in various spiritual and religious traditions. Most of these beliefs comprise an element of the unseen, supernatural, or something more than the reality that we can see from our own eyes. These different types of energies have been called spirit, soul, source, qi, and many other names. Basically, there's a belief that everything is energy, and science has interfered with presenting its verdict.

Let's have a look at the concept of energy in the different scientific eras of the past:

Newtonian Physics

Newtonian physics, also known as classical mechanics, is simply the explanation of mechanical events that involve forces acting on matter. It is named after perhaps one of the greatest scientists of all time, Sir Isaac Newton. At the end of the 17th century, Newtonian physics was considered the cornerstone of science. It described the physical laws that affect the motion of the physical bodies due to the influence of a system of forces. In this concept, the entire universe was perceived as some sort of a clockwork model. It also perceived human beings as some complex machinery. The only things that could be measured by scientific instruments and could be perceived through sense were considered as 'real.' The rest was termed as made-up nonsense created by primitive people with little to no education. The Newtonian world is the reality that can be experienced by using our five senses or, as one of my (still) skeptical friends would say: "I BELIEVE WHAT I CAN SEE."

The New Science

During the 20th century, the belief was altered again, as quantum physics was introduced to the world. This new concept accepted the fact that the entire universe, including us (humans), are made up of energy, not matter. The biggest contributors to the field of quantum mechanics were two German physicists, Max Planck, and Albert Einstein. In 1905, Einstein published a paper on a quantum-based theory that explained the photoelectric effect, which changed the perception of the entire scientific community on energy.

Quantum Physics

One of the fundamental beliefs of quantum physics is that there is no solid matter in the universe, and everything is made up of atoms. Atoms are not solid; in fact, they are made up of sub-atomic particles, electrons, protons, and neutrons.

Atoms that form solids are actually made up of 99.99 percent space between the sub-atomic particles – which means energy.

Since atoms are energy and they made up everything in the universe, it is proved that everything is energy. And if you now look at your body and you wonder whether this is also valid for you, then I can confirm that you are not an exception.

Niels Bohr, a brilliant Danish physicist, summed it up perfectly:

"If quantum mechanics hasn't profoundly shocked you, you haven't understood it yet. Everything we call real is made of things that cannot be regarded as real."

-Niels Bohr

Emotions = <u>E</u>nergy in <u>Motion</u>

It is pretty random to form any kind of connection between emotions and energy, but in reality, there is a lot of it. One of the greatest researchers on this topic these days is Dr. Joe Dispenza.

"If you think of a radio, you tune the circuitry to make it resonate with the frequency you want to receive. In the biological system, it's our nervous system that acts as a receiver to connect to information beyond our senses."

-Dr. Joe Dispenza

You might have wondered at a friend or loved one calling or texting the moment after you start thinking about them? Similarly, how can a mother sense that her child might be in trouble or some kind of distress despite being hundreds of miles away? Well, these events simply aren't coincidences, and there are actually three possibilities that make them happen. The first one is 'intuition.'

According to the definition of intuition in the Merriam Webster dictionary, "The power or faculty of attaining direct knowledge or cognition without evident rational thought and interference." In other words, direct knowledge is basically just a download of information from the unified field, surrounding us, into our brains. This occurs whenever we stop thinking and observing and go into a trance.

It almost feels like the brain pauses for a moment, and this pause enables other types of information to enter the nervous system. However, not everyone can decipher and understand the meaning of this information when they receive it. Even if someone manages to do so, they simply ignore it or refuse to believe in it. Mothers, on the other hand, tend to trust it more often. Everyone has access to this sort of information, but only a few of us are skilled enough to receive it with an open mind.

There is a different possibility to explain this phenomenon of connection; that is, people with a strong emotional bond between them are connected by an invisible field of information. Human beings might be made up of matter, but we are also full of energy and constantly emitting information into the world. However, this information can only be received by the people that are emotionally close to us. The best example to describe this phenomenon is that of a radio. The older models of the radio systems needed manual tuning to set to a particular frequency. Once you set it to the right frequency, you began receiving that channel. Similarly, there are billions of people on this planet, and every one of them is emitting information but at different frequencies. Once they are emotionally connected to each other, they start to understand the information that they receive.

There is also another explanation for this mysterious connection, and it is known as 'heart-centered energy.' Studies have revealed that when you operate at an elevated stage such as compassion, love, and gratitude, you start radiating these feelings around your body. This radiation field starts expanding, and people that are close to us start receiving this radiation.

Science still doesn't have a definite answer to how intuition works, but more and more studies are being conducted on the subject to find it out. However, we do know that it isn't magic.

"Perhaps now more than ever, it's so important for us to start each day from a greater level of awareness, a more heart-centered state of being, and from a place of wholeness."

-Dr. Joe Dizpenza

The energy that our bodies emit is not just limited to a person-to-person connection. Perhaps there is an even bigger impact of this energy emission.

For example, when we feel elevated emotions such as love, gratitude, or compassion, our hearts start beating at a particular frequency, which translates into a message. The heart also creates the largest electromagnetic field from the human body, which means researchers can extract significant data from it.

For the past decade, the scientific community has been busy studying the electromagnetic field generated by the human body and how it relates to the magnetic field of the Earth.

According to research conducted by HeartMath Institute, a solar and geomagnetic activity directly affects our autonomic nervous system. It also responds to changes that occur in the magnetic activity of the Earth and the sun. This study also suggested that our autonomous nervous system synchronizes with the magnetic fields that are varying in time and associated with geomatics field-line resonances and Schumann resonances. Schumann resonances can be considered as earth's 'heartbeat'[1].

The effect on our energy levels when combining clear intention with a strong emotion was proven with a fascinating experiment carried out by the French scientist Rene Peoc'h. He wanted to study the possibility how intention might operate in our world. He started with a computerized robot set up as a random event generator. Set lose in an area, the robot turned right half the time and left half the time, thereby covering the area equally over time.

This is perfectly in keeping with the idea of a random generator. Then he allowed some chicks to imprint on the computerized robot as if it were their mother right after

---

[1] McCarty, R. Atkinson, M. Stolc, V. Alabdulgader, A.A. Vainoras, A. Ragulskis, M. (2017). Synchronization of Human Autonomic Nervous System Rhythms with Geomagnetic Activity in Human Subjects. MDPI. Retrieved from: https://www.mdpi.com/1660-4601/14/7/770

hatching. So, the chicks bonded with the robot creating an energetic bond on their part (at least), and hence the chicks followed the robot no matter where it went. Once the chicks had imprinted, Peoc'h put them in a cage where they could see the robot but not go to it. What do you think happened?

If you hold a materialistic (Newtonian) view of the world, you would say nothing. The random event generator can't be affected by the minds of the chicks. It's ridiculous! But the pattern of movement of the robot clustered near the chicks' cage. No longer was the robot moving randomly, but now it had gravitated near the babies. Cool experiment, right? And easily replicated. The larger question becomes if baby chicks can influence objects around them, how much influence do we have?

If you still think this is impossible, it's your choice. Always remember that you are the master of your thoughts and this comes with responsibility. If you think Quantum physics is not within your reach – so be it. But if you think it is the best realization in your life you tab into the unlimited possibilities that Quantum physics has to offer. After having studied and applied these principles I am convinced that it works and today I can say: "I CAN SEE WHAT I

BELIEVE." I don´t want to close this section without making a reference to the powerful work of the group Fearless Soul. They created a great video on the concept of energy and what impact the unlimited field of energy can have on us.

I quote an extract here to summarize what we have learned so far about the beauty of a balanced energy level. Enjoy!

"You are ENERGY!

Do you really understand this, do you really get how you are energy?

Energy is flowing through you right now.

Energy is around you right now.

You are moving in energy.

You are driving your car in energy.

You are breathing in and breathing out energy.

Your body is filled with energy.

The thoughts you are thinking, your feelings, your happiness, your confusion is energy.

The blood that is pumping around your body filling every cell with oxygen is energy.

Every part of you that is growing, your hair, your nails, if you are a little person, your limbs, use energy to grow.

What you eat is energy, what you say, what comes out of your mouth is energy.

What you look at is energy, what you pay attention to gives it more energy.

If you watch things on TV or online you are giving your energy to what you watch.

You are aligning your energy with those things.

ENERGY FLOWS WHERE ATTENTION GOES.

What are you really giving your energy to?

It is your choice what you are giving your energy to.

It is your FREE WILL to choose. WHAT ARE YOU CHOOSING?

What does your energy look like, what does it feel like?

Your energy is flowing in directions whether you want it to or not.

Your thoughts and your feelings direct your energy….."

Principles of Abundance to Enhance Your Life

"The key to abundance is meeting limited circumstances with unlimited thoughts."

-Marianne Williamson

Lack of abundance is one of the problems that are holding you back in life and in order to let it flow into the other areas of your life. You need to shift your mindset. You will eventually find out that the more you focus on what you do have you will find an abundance of time, money and opportunities that come your way.

Here are some of the abundance principles and some empowering exercises that can help you shift your mindset.

Stop Feeling Like a Victim When It Comes to Money

People who are blessed with wealth often boast about how they created their own life. While people who struggle financially tend to victimize themselves. Following are some of the steps that you can take in order to get rid of the victim mentality when it comes to money:

Step 1: Write down the names of the people and situations that prevent you from making money in life. If you are unable to write down anything, then it means you are completely responsible for whatever happens in your life.

Step 2: Tell yourself that money is important to you because it actually is. People who struggle to make sufficient money often develop a belief that money isn't important to them which is one of the main reasons why their struggles continue to grow. If you tell a person that she is not important to you, then she would surely avoid hanging out near you. Same things happen to money when you do not consider it important anymore.

Step 3: Eliminate complaining from your life completely. Of course, you cannot do that immediately. Therefore, try not to complain for a whole day first and then start adding days as you progress. Complaining about everything only makes you lazy and less motivated to do anything in your life, because it gives you (bad) excuses for not achieving your goals.

Your Beliefs Create Experiences

If you start believing that you do not deserve anything good in this world, then that is exactly what's going to happen to you. Similarly, if you become optimistic and view everything positively, you are going to achieve everything that you work towards. That's because your beliefs are pictured in your experiences. I would like to share a story with you that happened to me after I started working for a new employer. I am working in sales and business development and after a couple of month in the office I was working on a strategic (future) client that is very important for the firm. A few months later, still working on getting this prospect over the finish line, I had a chat with one of my colleagues of the sales support team. He is a very rational guy and did an analysis of my case. He told me that we will never win this client based on all the key success indicators he analyzed and I should not waste too much energy on that anymore.

I only looked at him and said to him that I will respond to his analysis once the prospect is a client. Another 3 months later we won the business and my colleague approached me to congratulate me for the win started by saying the magic

words: "I still CAN'T BELIEVE that we won this business."
And I answered: "Now you know why we won it, because I
never had any doubts about bringing this client home." In
other words you always need to be conscious about your
thoughts even if people crossing your way who don't share
your view. My thoughts and beliefs create my reality. So, I
better be mindful what I think, or as a friend once said to me:
"Be careful what you wish for…!"

Shift Your Belief from Scarcity to a Belief in Abundance

One of the biggest mistakes we make is that we tend to
think about everything in human terms. This limits our
potential due to human constraints. In order to have
unlimited potential, we need to shift our belief to a higher
power as a source of abundance. This higher power can be
in the form of Mother Nature, God or Spirit, any entity that
is not bound any limits. Shifting your belief to abundance
will automatically get rid of scarcity.

You create abundance by believing that you live in a
world of more than enough. Your perception becomes your
reality. Sounds familiar? Exactly, it is the law of attraction
in action. This is the reason why a belief in abundance (there

is plenty for everyone!) over scarcity (there is only so much and I am afraid to get my fair share) makes such a big difference in our ability to develop a mind-set necessary to live a joyful and fulfilled life. If you want to enter the universe of abundance you need a key to open the door. This key is called gratefulness which means you first need to appreciate all the things you have already achieved and attracted into your life. This includes all your desires and wishes you still aspire or as Denzel Washington once wisely said: "Say thank you in advance, for what is already yours!"

It's crucial to understand that we are only a tiny part of the entirety. So, why not reconnect to this ultimate intelligence, call it the source, Mother Nature, god or simply abundance.

Developing Limitless Mental Strength

"The ability to continue moving when you are feeling scared, fearful or lazy is the sign of true mental strength."

-Matthew Donnelly

The importance of mental strength should never be ignored. It allows people to be more efficient, productive and conscientious of the task that they are doing. Good mental strength has a direct impact on educational achievements at all levels. Similarly, it also has to do everything when a person enters the professional world. Unless you have good mental strength at the helm, you won't be able to conquer all your goals and desires. One of the best ways to boost your mental strength is through 'Stoicism." Stoicism is an ancient Greek philosophy that was introduced by Zeno of Citium. Zeno was an incredibly rich merchant who lost all of his wealth and power in a short span of life. Instead of spiraling down into depression, Zeno decided to study philosophy and started reading about great minds such as Heraclitus and Socrates. He would then go on to create stoicism which would turn out to be a revolutionary philosophy.

According to stoicism, *"The path to happiness for humans is found in accepting this moment as it presents itself, by not allowing ourselves to be controlled by our desire for pleasure or our fear of pain, by using our minds to understand the world around us and to do our part in nature's plan, and by working together and treating other fairly and justly."*

-Stefanov, I (2018), 7 Principles of Stoicism for Limitless
Mental Strength

Here are the five principles of stoicism that can help you improve your mental strength.

You Only Have Power Over Your Mind

You need to understand that the only thing you have power over is your own mind and not external events. Life is full of bad moments, and no one can live through it with 100 percent happiness. Imagine you are running late for work and notice that your car has a flat tire. Majority of the people will get furious at this moment and may even curse to vent out their frustration. However, this behavior will not change their tire. According to stoicism, you only have two choices at this moment – either change your tire or just keep standing there and build your blood pressure up.

You cannot control the events that happen to you in the outside world, but you can control your mind-set which helps you stay calm and resolve difficult situations instead of complaining about them. Never forget that there is no one single reality on this planet. Instead, you form your reality by simply perceiving and interpreting the circumstances. So, if your reality is only a mind game, why not defining the rules in your best interest and play your biggest game.

Death Makes Life Worth More

No matter what your beliefs are as a human being, but each and every person on the planet can agree on one point, and that is death. Death is inevitable, therefore, ignoring it is just pointless. One of the Stoics' exercises includes picturing the day of their death. This exercise makes them appreciate every single day of life (either good or bad) because they accept the fact that they are mortals. This is one point that differentiates stoicism from all the other philosophies. Your time is limited, and any day can be your last. So, are you wasting your time? Stop thinking and do something to live your life to the fullest. Just ask yourself this question, "If today was my last day, how would I spend it?"

By the way, while I'm writing this, I'm just back from the funeral of my mother in law, which reminded me again to the finality of death. So, what's holding you back from living the most abundant life while you stroll over this wonderful planet?

Food Is Not For Pleasure

Stoics have a firm belief that food should never be a source of pleasure. Instead, it should be seen as a fuel necessary to stay alive in the best way possible. Eating foods that are beneficial for your health is the best thing you can do for improving your mental strength. In the end, your body is nothing more than transformed food consumed over your life. It is like building a robust house, you need good quality concrete to build something that last for long.

Hardship Is Good

"The Impediment to action advances action. What stands in the way becomes the way."

-Marcus Aurelius

It is important to be grateful for the hard times as they let you appreciate the good ones. You can express your frustration when things are going south or you simply take it as a great opportunity to build your character.

Stoics never shy away from hardships. Instead, they love to face them because they consider it as an opportunity to practice their virtue. They also believe that acting bravely and morally right in the face of adversity is the highest form of dignity.

Small Things Matter the Most

You no longer need millions of dollars, a gigantic house and multiple cars to satisfy yourself once you start appreciating small things in life. This is the founding principle of stoicism. There is absolutely nothing wrong in dreaming about a perfect life, but there is no certainty of when you are going to achieve. So, if you fail to appreciate small things in life, you will be frustrated and may also give up on your dreams altogether.

At his point I would like to introduce the idea of the compound effect. A concept that will be explained in more detail later in the book. For now it is important to understand that it is not about the big bang moment that we all seek to success. It is the small, insignificant step as a stand-alone action that makes the difference.

The compound effect explains the magic of doing these little but effective actions in a consistent manner. Going to the dentist two times per year won't help your teeth much; it is brushing your teeth two times per day every day that will maintain your winner smile. Stoicism is not just an ancient Greek philosophy that is not relevant anymore, but it is a way of life that many people still choose. It is the ultimate formula for developing patience and mental strength that is necessary to succeed in life.

We have now discussed the preconditions of an accelerated life. With that, and using the picture of a lighthouse under construction we have defined where we stand in life and hence where we want to build our lighthouse. A place that can carry a strong building and that is exposed enough to spend the guiding light for people in need. In the next chapter we will start building the foundation of our lighthouse.

Chapter 3
Building the Foundation

"It is not the beauty of the building you should look at; it's the construction that will stand the test of time."

-David Allan Coe

After going through the previous chapter, which was completely based on awakening and turning point of your life, you should be familiar with the importance to turn your life around. The best way to do that is by building your life from scratch. It is never too late to start over again as long as you have breath in your lungs and blood pumping through your veins. You are good to go.

The best analogy to consider when it comes to building the foundation of your life is the construction of an actual building, house or any other structure of shelter. However, since this book is named after a lighthouse, we are going to select it as a particular example to demonstrate how to construct a lighthouse from the ground up.

So, what do you typically do when you want to build a lighthouse? Well, the first thing you do is look for a high altitude ground that looks over the ocean. After selecting the perfect construction venue, you begin working on the foundation of the lighthouse. The foundation is the most important part of the lighthouse as the entire structure's stability, and life depends on it. This is why a strong foundation requires solid concrete and steel to hold the structure for several generations firmly.

A strong foundation is the reason why a lighthouse can stand against strong winds and powerful ocean waves. Regardless of how extreme the weather is, the lighthouse firmly stands on its spot and guides ships and airplanes.

Building the lighthouse of your life also requires a solid foundation. However, instead of the physical materials, that are needed to build a literal lighthouse, you need strong values to build your personal life up. These values comprise for example of:

- Honesty
- Transparency
- Helpfulness

- Gratefulness
- Consistency & Courage
- Integrity
- Belief
- Love

Why are these basic values so important for your life? These essential building blocks of life are putting you in a position to validate every situation in your life. A set of strong values works like a gatekeeper. It only lets such behavior pass that supports your way of life so that you can live your life on your own terms. To do so, you need to define your personal, most important key terms. The above list should only act as a catalyst that provokes further inner discussion with yourself. So, find a quiet place where you can reflect on what really matters to you and write your own list of values and believes. Let's kick this inner work off by discussing a few main values in the following.

Honesty

If you are looking to build your life's foundation, then the first value that you might want to consider is honesty. Being honest to yourself and with all the people that surround you will not only bring peace in your life but will also help you in re-constructing your personality as the better version of your previous self.

We all had been in situations in which we had to decide to either tell the truth and hence live with the consequences, or find excuses, lie about what happened and even blame someone else. This reaction is human and very tempting, but not honest. The next time when you catch yourself while considering to cut *"ethical corners"* you might want to think about this little anecdote.

The story is told that one day Frederick the Great, King of Prussia, visited a prison and talked with each of the inmates. There were endless tales of innocence, of misunderstood motives, and of exploitation. Finally the king stopped at the cell of a convict who remained silent.

"Well," remarked Frederick, *"I suppose you are an innocent victim too?"*

"No, sir, I'm not," replied the man. *"I'm guilty and deserve my punishment."*

Turning to the warden, the king said, *"Here, release this rascal before he corrupts all these fine innocent people in here!"*

Transparency

Transparency is another strong value that is required for building the lighthouse of yourself. One of the best practices you can do to be transparent with yourself is by keeping a record of your life's achievements and failures. Keeping a diary/journal or writing a blog are some of the primary examples of personal record keeping. However, you need to make sure that you portray yourself with complete transparency in this record keeping.

Being transparent with yourself reveals all your flaws and shortcomings. In this way, you can focus on improving them during the building process of your life. It also helps you in developing a perspective on who you are. So, when you face any challenge in your life, you can remind yourself of the time when you overcame an even bigger hurdle. Similarly, when you feel that life is moving in slow motion, then you can recall the time when patience helped you succeed. Your past decisions can be used as motivation to figure out the problems of the present simply by being transparent to yourself. Transparency means letting your shield down and allowing others to experience you as you really are. It needs a good portion of courage to show others the real you but this courage pays off as you don't have to play a role anymore. With that, people can interact with you naturally and hence the communication moves away from the superficial level of mere acting to a highly satisfying level of real connection and exchange of emotions.

"A lack of transparency results in distrust and a deep sense of insecurity."

-Dalai Lama

Helpfulness

Being helpful to yourself and others is a key to happiness and success which makes it an important ingredient for building the foundation of your life. Some people are confused by the fact that someone else can help them to succeed in life.

To address this doubt, here are some of the reasons why helping others is beneficial for you.

It Makes You Feel Great

Helping a person in need gives an unexplainable sense of satisfaction to you. It makes you feel good about yourself, and there is a scientific reason for why this happens. Studies have shown that when people donate to charity or help a homeless person, their mesolimbic system is triggered. It releases the feel-good chemicals which give them a feeling of pleasure. This feeling is termed as "helper's high"[2].

You Become Optimistic and Positive

Helping others is also linked with a change in the helper's attitude and outlook. Experts have revealed that performing acts of kindness improves your mood and makes you positive and optimistic[3].

It Boosts Your Morale

Helping others motivates you to the point where you feel like you can take on the world. It leaves the feeling that you

---

[2] Der Linden, SV (2013). The Helper's High. Princeton. Retrieved from: https://scholar.princeton.edu/sites/default/files/slinden/files/helpershigh.pdf
[3] Castillo, S (2012). 13 Ways to Be Nicer. Prevention. Retrieved from: https://www.prevention.com/life/a20447046/doing-kind-acts-reduces-anxiety-study/

have accomplished something and have been rewarded for it greatly. According to a survey by the United Health Group, people who do volunteer work tend to feel more empowered that those who avoid it[4].

You Will Find Your Inner Peace

Helping others also relieves stress and clears your head. According to a study conducted by the United Health Group, a group of people volunteered over a 12-month-period to do some charity work. Almost 78 percent of those people reported that these activities lowered their stress levels[5].

"There is no exercise better for the heart than reaching down and lifting people up."

-John Holmes

---

[4] United Health Group (2013). Doing Good is Good for You. Retrieved from: https://www.unitedhealthgroup.com/content/dam/UHG/PDF/2013/UNH-Health-Volunteering-Study.pdf
[5] United Health Group (2013). Doing Good is Good for You. Retrieved from: https://www.unitedhealthgroup.com/content/dam/UHG/PDF/2013/UNH-Health-Volunteering-Study.pdf

Gratefulness

It is pretty easy to be ungrateful nowadays. It is also easy to desire for things we don't have and ignore the ones we do have. It's not until we lose everything that we realize the worth of what we had.

Life is full of ups and downs, and you might not be at your best at the current moment but, you should be grateful for what you have right now and strive for better things.

Following are some of the reasons how gratitude can help you in building the lighthouse of your life.

It Shifts Your Focus

Life is all about focus. Wherever your focus is, you will move in that direction. If you live in the state of negativity, you will see more of that. It is very easy to see things in a negative manner because negativity is stitched into the fabric of society.

However, it is equally easy to see things in a positive light as well. If you have ever met an overly positive person in your life (remember what I wrote about my mother), then you might find this fact true. Some people always tend to see positivity in everything. Even when things aren't going according to their plan, they somehow manage to find some silver lining in it. You can incorporate positivity in your life by just being grateful. It shifts your focus, and you start seeing things positively. You appreciate the beauty in everything around you. Your living standard changes as you move from living in a state of lacking to living in a state of profusion.

Still, you need to understand that this shift in focus doesn't happen overnight. It might be easy, but it requires time. You can achieve it by simply creating a habit of writing down all of the things that you are grateful for on a daily basis.

Last but not least when you are in a state of being grateful there is no space left for being worried or angry. So, you have the choice to start your days with being grateful for what you are and what you have achieved already. If you do so abundance will take care of itself.

"When you arise in the morning, think of what a precious privilege it is to be alive, to breathe, to think, to enjoy and to love."

-Marcus Aurelius

It Makes You Happier

Many studies have confirmed that being grateful can result in happiness. Two psychologists, Dr. Michael E. McCullough from the University of Miami, and Dr. Robert A. Emmons, dedicated the better part of their careers in studying the effects of gratitude on people[6].

In one of their studies, they asked a group of people to write down the things that they were grateful for. Another group of people was assigned the task of writing down the things that didn't make them happy.

The results revealed that people that wrote about things that they were grateful for were happier and optimistic when compared to the other group that wrote down negativity. It's natural to feel happier about life when you are grateful for

---

[6]Harvard Health Publishing (2019). Giving thanks can make you happier. Retrieved from: https://www.health.harvard.edu/healthbeat/giving-thanks-can-make-you-happier

everything. That's because you are thankful for the things you have rather than the things you don't.

It Improves Your Quality of Life

Gratitude directly affects your wellness, mental and physical health, emotional fortitude and spiritual aptitude.

Many studies have proved that gratitude is linked directly with the fulfillment of life and people who are grateful for everything are more satisfied in their lives[7].

It Eliminates You Inner Fears

Being grateful can reduce your fears because it is difficult to be afraid and thankful at the same time. When we live in a state of fear, we expect the worst possible scenarios and keep thinking about our end which we assume won't be so well. But you can overcome fear by being grateful. If we are fully thankful for all that we have, including all our

---

[7] Alex M. Wood, Maltby, J. Joseph, S. (2008). Gratitude uniquely predicts satisfaction with life: Incremental validity above the domains and facets of the five-factor model. Science Direct. Retrieved from: https://www.health.harvard.edu/healthbeat/giving-thanks-can-make-you-happier

problems, fear has little room for us to live in. We live in a state of lacking instead of abundance. If we are afraid of the things that put us in a state of scarcity, such as not having enough money to pay our bills or to put our food on our tables, we stay limited to only achieving our material needs. However, being grateful puts you in abundance. If you begin believing that at this very moment you have everything you need and don't worry about what you don't or won't have at some point in the future, you will feel thankful and attract even more abundance in your life.

It Encourages You to Accomplish Your Goals

You can literally achieve anything to which you put your mind to when you set goals the right way. Being grateful can change your life by encouraging you to achieve these goals.

As long as your mind, body, and spirit are happy, healthy and sound, you can achieve your objectives without too many distractions from others. But if you're not happy with the current state of affairs, it's more difficult to push you forward, because you're unhappy with this state of negativity and lacking.

How can you tirelessly push for goals that can take years to come about when you are focused on things that are wrong with your life? It doesn't work. Instead, you tend to distract yourself, waste your time and pursue actions that prevent you from achieving your goals.

It Gives You Peace of Mind

When you are truly grateful for everything you have, you develop an inner belief. This belief provides you with the peace of mind that doesn't exist when you are living with expectations of certain things. People who bring down others for the sole purpose of their personal advancement are feeble-minded individuals who often fail in life.

For those who remain humble, although endowed by their meteoric growth, fame or stardom, there is a level of respect that no one can deny them. Humility is certainly one of the prevailing qualities of many of the world's most successful people because they had to withstand and recover from their sufferings and failures.

They were grateful that they didn't take things for granted because they had to go through oceans of pain to achieve what they got. The victory of the successful people who have endured a lot of failure before trying out a sweet success is characterized by a certain humility and empathy.

But everything begins with an attitude of gratefulness that helps bring tranquility in your life. Success was developed from this platform. Nothing is achievable through craftiness or deceitful conduct. Only good will, positive attitude and the will to make the world more valuable, work in the best way.

"A grateful heart is a beginning of greatness. It is an expression of humility. It is a foundation for the development of such virtues as prayer, faith, courage, contentment, happiness, love, and well-being."

-James E. Faust

Integrity

The Cambridge dictionary describes integrity as the quality of being honest and having strong moral principles that one refuses to change. Having integrity means doing the right thing in a reliable way. It's a personality trait that we admire, since it means a person has a moral compass that doesn't waver. It literally means having "wholeness" of character, just as an integer is a "whole number" with no fractions. Physical objects like the foundations of a lighthouse can display integrity, too — if you're going up the staircase of a rock solid lighthouse that resists the storm and the waves easily, you don't question its structural integrity.

Consistency & Courage

Courage plays a big role when building the life you desire. The best values not applied consistently are simply an alibi only pretending that you know what really matters to you. It takes huge mental strength to resist the temptation of quick short-term wins and stick to your overarching principles and values to win the game of life in the long-term. Think about life as running a marathon. It is the small but effective steps that you do in a very consistent manner that makes you succeed.

It is the courage that convinces you to give it a try even though it feels like standing in front of the Mount Everest. You need to trust your basic values and then you start building your base camps consistently, one by one, until you reach the peek. Never forget that even the longest and most difficult ventures have a starting point, something that starts with one single step. If you wonder where your unlimited power and conviction to succeed is coming from, you might want to continue with the next base value.

"A journey of a thousand miles begins with a single step."

-Laozi, from the Tao Te Ching

Belief

We all start out as innocent children with a heart full of high hopes and ambitions. Some of us want to be an astronaut, while some dream to become a rock star. However, reality soon hits us when we step into the practical world, and we are taught that whatever we dreamed as kids is just impractical to aim for in real life - remember my story about keeping both boots on the ground. Although nothing is impossible to achieve if you are highly convinced of your idea, most people still give up on their dreams when they face the first signs of head winds. One of the major reasons most people tend to abandon their aspirations is their lack of self-belief. When it comes to success, nothing is more influential than believing in yourself that you can achieve something outstanding. In fact, self-belief holds more importance than talent, intelligence, background, or just about any other trait. People who have self-belief are happier, healthier, and more resilient and motivated than those who lack self-belief.

There are many things that hinder your self-belief such as your parents, upbringing, society and environment that you grew in and also how people treated you. It is the conditioning process that we all went through and makes us "fit in." However, a lack of self-belief is not directly related to the skill, talent or ability of a person. In fact, it is more related to our perception. I would like to share the example of how Indian Elephants are trained to stay with their owners, the so called "mahouts" to demonstrate how conditioned we, the human beings, are.

They take them when they are still small and tie a strong rope around their leg and attach the rope to a secure pole. The baby elephants naturally try to walk away and are stopped by the rope. They pull and push and twist and turn and eventually figure out that they just aren't strong enough to break free of their shackles, so they stop resisting and just stay where they are.

The next time they tie up the baby elephants they try to break away once again, pulling on the rope to see if they can go free. When they figure out that once again it is futile, they stop pulling and settle down and stay where they are. This process repeats over and over again until the moment the elephants stay still the moment they are attached to the rope.

The elephant becomes so accustomed to being held by the rope that even when they grow up and have the strength to break free, they don't believe in their strength anymore and stay put.

It seems to me that we, the adults, have also learned the rules of society, the dos and especially the don't dos and over time forgot about our strengths and the belief that we can achieve extraordinary things in life. My recommendation: Strip off the rope, remind yourself of your incredible capabilities, think big and believe in your dreams. All of us have suffered, made mistakes and gone through failures in our lives. Even the most successful people that you know had to go through some tough times to be where they are now. All of these disappointments can affect your self-confidence and also the belief in your own abilities. It is all down to you whether you let these down times affect your self-belief negatively or use it as a motivation to strengthen your self-confidence in your abilities.

To understand the wonders of self-confidence, the following is a famous story that might motivate you to do better for yourself than what you are doing right now[8]:

A young business executive was going through a lot of troubles with his company in terms of debts, and there was simply no way out for him.

Creditors were closing in on him, and suppliers were furiously demanding payments. To relieve some work-related stress, the executive decided to head to the park. He found a bench and sat on it. His head was in his hands, and he was brainstorming the ways to save his company from bankruptcy.

---

[8]Ed De Costa (2012). Believing is seeing: Self-confidence in action. Retrieved from: https://eddecosta.com/believing-is-seeing-self-confidence-in-action/

Suddenly, an old man approached him and said, *"I can see that you are worried about something, young man."* The business executive replied with a nod and started telling his story to the old man. After listening to his troubles, the old man calmly took out his checkbook and asked the name of the executive. He wrote him a check, placed it in his hands and said, *"Use this money to resolve your issues and then meet me exactly here one year later to return it."* After handing him the check, the old man got up and went his way without saying goodbye.

The young executive then stared at the check and was astonished to see that it was for $500,000 and was signed by John D. Rockefeller (back then, one of the richest men in the world).

The young executive was ecstatic to see that because that amount of money was more than enough to eliminate his company's financial issues. But he also thought about returning the money a year later. Encouraged by the trust of Rockefeller, he decided not to use the check immediately and instead stored it in a safe place. He started working harder than before, with renewed self-confidence this time. He knew at the back of his mind that he had the ultimate tool to resolve all his problems in an instant which reduced his worries and he worked hard without any stress. Within a few months, the young executive was able to take his company from the brink of bankruptcy to start making profits. Days passed and exactly one year later, the executive returned to the same park with the uncashed check in his hand to find the old man. After waiting for a while on the same bench, he finally saw the old man walking towards him. Just as he was about to approach him a nurse came running and shouting. She grabbed the old man by the arm and said, *"I am so glad I caught you!"* She then turned to the business executive and said, *"I am so sorry if he bothered you. He has dementia, and he keeps on escaping from the nursing home. He also goes around handing checks to random people and claiming to be John D. Rockefeller."*

The nurse then escorted the old man away, and the executive stood stunned and speechless. He just realized that he had been working hard only due to his own self-confidence which he had gotten through a check for half a million dollars. He had this self-confidence this whole time even if he didn't have the money to solve all his problems!

The above story may or may not be true, but it gives out a great message about the wonders you can achieve by just believing in your abilities. We should never forget that we have everything necessary to solve our issues and get back on track inside of us all the time. There are many ways to develop a strong belief in yourself, but it requires an incredible amount of time and effort. It is also really important to keep in mind that your past should not dictate your future life. What really matters is how you act today.

Following are some of the most empowering ways to develop self-confidence and start believing in yourself.

List Down All Your Past Accomplishments

One of the ways people destroy their self-belief is by reliving all their past failures and embarrassing moments from time to time. These bad times often prevent you from taking risks in life, and you end up losing self-confidence because of that. What you should be doing instead is focus on your success and accomplishments from the past.

Making a list of all the positive accomplishments in life, regardless of how big and small they are, will not only boost your self-confidence but will also astonish you when you realize how many personal accomplishments you had overlooked so far in your life. To use these past achievements as motivation, try reading them every day to remind yourself that you can achieve anything, just like you did in the past.

Ask People for Positive Feedback

Most of us tend to surround ourselves with the people that we love and care about a lot. These people also stay close to us because they see something inside us that they like and it makes them feel good to be around us.

Your friends, family, boyfriend/girlfriend are the best people to get positive feedback from. Therefore, you need to ask them about the things they find interesting in you. Ask them about all your positive traits, skills and talents, and you will most likely receive positive feedback from them that will boost your belief in yourself.

This activity is really important because most of the people tend to be really critical of themselves. Therefore, positive reinforcement from other people can be empowering and will also have a huge impact on your self-belief and confidence.

Take One Step At A Time – but do it consistently

One of the most popular traits of humans is impatience. If we desire something, we want it right now. However, life doesn't always work this way. If you want a candy bar, you can go to the store and get it instantly, but if you want to build a (light) house, it just doesn't happen the same way. Therefore, you need to learn to be patient if you want to build the foundation of your new life with the help of self-belief.

One of the basic rules of life is that you always have to start from the bottom. Look at some of the most successful people in the world and then look at their humble beginnings. They didn't achieve what they have right now overnight, instead, they had to go through many sleepless nights and gruesome working hours to accomplish their goals.

The co-founder of Apple Computers (Apple Inc.), Steve Jobs, started his company in his garage. He worked for years before his company would start making him any profit and eventually would make him a billionaire. What drove him was self-confidence and belief in himself that he could revolutionize the world of computing by taking on giants like IBM. He managed to do that, and though he may not be around to see it, Apple Inc. is the biggest tech company in the world today. It might seem like your life is stagnant right now and whatever efforts you are putting in to make it better are being wasted then you are wrong. Be patient, give it some time, and you will soon start seeing the benefits of everything you are doing. Bringing patience in your life will bolster your self-belief and help you in building a strong foundation of the lighthouse of your life.

A successful life is nothing else but small, effective and consistently carried out steps strung to a sustainable chain of invincible actions. Darren Hardy calls it the *compound effect* and uses the following example.

Let's assume you want to lose weight and get into a better shape. You ask a nutritionist for a diet and sign up for a program at your local gym. You clean up the fridge, fill it with healthy stuff and invest even in a new sports gear. You follow the diet for a day and go to the gym and exercise for four hours. After your successful first day you jump on the scale and....no change! Disappointed but still motivated you start the second day, you follow your diet and as four hours of training obviously didn't make an impact you exercise for five ours. You check your weight after day two and... again no improvement. Now you start getting frustrated, because after all your efforts you expected to see the first results but this is not how life works. It is not about massive actions that lead to a leap in performance. Life is about small, incremental changes that you implement in your daily routines that make the difference.

I'm not sure whether you have realized that you are practicing this technique already by, for example, cleaning your teeth every day, two times, for two minutes. Why not leave it with visiting the dentist twice a year and hoping for the best in between?

Overcome Your Fears As You Did in the Past

A lack of self-belief and confidence can instill fear in your life, and you start thinking about how worthless your life is and that you are not good enough to achieve something. You start fearing the consequences of failure, and this is why you refuse to try hard as well.

This fear can be paralyzing and may also prevent your progress towards a successful life. One way to counteract this fear is by thinking about the time you conquered one of your fears in the past. Think about how good it felt when you overcame that fear and was afraid ever again. It could simply be fear of drowning in water when you were little, and you finally overcame it by learning how to swim. Or it could be a big moment in your life when you finally managed to gather enough courage to ask out your crush on a dinner date. A good way to remember these accomplishments is by writing them down.

What's the purpose of fear at all?

The mind magnifies danger to protect us from taking risks. This is an old, deeply embedded way of surviving and made perfectly sense when we still lived in caves 50,000 years ago, looking at a saber-toothed tiger from afar and deciding to flee. Nowadays, there are not so many saber-toothed tigers around anymore, even though there are people surrounding us that make us wonder whether some of them survived. But in reality, the risk of failure is not as big as it seems and once you overcome it, it feels like a small hurdle from the past. Mark Twain summed it perfectly by saying:

"I have spent most of my life worrying about things that never happened."

Whenever you have clarity on what you want to achieve next and you feel fear rising up and taking control, think about the following image. Regard your life as a (light) house with an unlimited number of rooms. So, far you have probably only explored a few of these rooms (opportunities). While approaching a door to the next room towards the unknown you will feel the fear caused by uncertainty, not knowing what's waiting behind the door. Use this feeling as an indicator that you are on the right track. Instead of giving in to the temptation to pull out, you resist and push yourself out of your comfort zone.

Never forget the reason why you go towards the unknown, why you leave your comfort zone – it is your inner wisdom that makes you understand that life happens on the other side of your fear. Once you have done it you are capable of translating fear into curiosity. Never stay put, never let fear control your life. Always regard the unknown as opportunity to build your character or as one of my heroes once wisely said:

"Named must your fear be before banish it you can."

-Yoda, Star Wars – The Empire Strikes Back

Celebrate Your Wins

It is really important to pat yourself on the back every now and then for the progress that you make towards your goal. No matter if the feedback you receive from others is positive, if you don't appreciate yourself then you will never achieve self-belief in life. It doesn't matter how small your achievement is. It requires appreciation because you actually made an effort instead of doing nothing. For example, if you ate healthy today because you want to lose weight in the future then congratulate yourself. If you walked for 5 minutes because you want to start exercising every day, then celebrate it. Focus on what you accomplish rather than what you did not.

Develop a new habit of maintaining a *success journal* and keep writing your daily wins in it to track your progress. List all the small victories that you accomplished and then feel good about yourself, because: You deserve it! This practice is extremely powerful and can boost your self-confidence. You will start believing in yourself again by doing it.

Stop Complaining

We all have some people in our lives that are always

whining and complaining about almost everything that happens in their lives. These people also tend to put the blame of their failures on others, and this is why they never progress ahead in life. When you complain about things going wrong, you are focusing on the negative side of the situation instead of what's right. This focus amplifies the negativity and affects your self-confidence. Having an optimistic thought helps you change your mindset and improves your confidence, and you start believing in the fact that things will eventually get better.

It is like what I have explained above. Life is like driving a car. Get seated on the driver seat, take the steering wheel and hence the responsibility for where you go. By doing so you are the owner and architect of your life, no one else can do this for you. So, buckle up and enjoy the ride!

In the end, you don't want to be rich. You want to be happy in life. Although many people have been convinced by mass media and society that being rich leads to happiness, this is not always the case. Money can certainly help you in achieving your goals, to provide for your future or to make your life more enjoyable. However, it doesn't guarantee any happiness. Happiness comes from the values of your life!

Values that are well thought through and applied consistently.

The values that we have discussed here can only give you a kick-start. Make up your mind which values are most important for you and write them down. These values are creating a very powerful foundation to start rebuilding your life. Think like an artist and be inspired by e.g., innovative architects and think out of the ordinary. Have you ever seen houses created by e.g., Friedensreich Hunderwasser?

"If one person dreams alone, it is only a dream. When many people dream together, it's the beginning of a new reality."

-Friedensreich Hunderwasser

The new foundation of life you're working on isn't driven by financial gain, but by values. These values are what allow you to develop a unique worldview and perspective that works for you.

Here is another one, undoubtedly the strongest of all.

Love

In his book *The LOLA-Principle, or The Perfectness of the World*, René Egli talks about how every problem has a solution. There's no issue in the world that can't be resolved, as long as you reshape your worldview to encapsulate the problem. Every human being thinks that they want free will, but are then consumed by the implications of it. The fact of the matter is that human beings have unlimited potential. Everything is energy/vibrations, and that means that everything can be transformed – from positive to negative and from negative to positive. It all depends on your worldview.

There is no such thing as an objective world. Rather, the world is purely a subjective interpretation. You've never made a mistake in your life; instead, you've learned. By learning, you become wise or, sometimes you win and sometimes you learn.

As René says, every problem has a solution. And that solution is love. Love is the answer to all problems. Make love a part of your worldview, and watch as your problems become easier to resolve. There's nothing mystical or esoteric about this to René. It's no new religion.

It's just Life.

Having finished this chapter we have built a rock solid foundation for our lighthouse. We are approaching the next floor by discussing the golden life rules. Rules that we want to master on our way towards abundance and joy.

Chapter 4
Golden Life Rules

Chapters 2 has helped guiding us on the path to achieving awareness of what it is that matters to us, as well as what we stand for in terms of our purpose in this world. In Chapter 3, we built an understanding of what values are important to us and agreed on certain assumptions, some fundamental principles that we need to understand to define the framework in which we are moving. In effect, we've walked up the stairs to the first floor in the lighthouse.

Now, in Chapter 4, we're going to get to the second floor. We've understood what we have to change internally – our convictions and our worldview. It's time to get tactical and figure out the rules of changing the internal world so we can drive our way to a successful life. For this, we need to understand the rules of the game called life.

Before we really delve into the Golden Life rules, let's quickly look at one of the most basic yet most effective ones: *keep it simple*. As modern humans, we've been wired to expect everything to be intricate and complicated, but that is not really the case. Everything in life is just an interpretation of it, your interpretation. It is up to us to interpret it the way we want, the way it serves us best, to magnify the good things in life and let go of the struggles.

It's All About Mindfulness

If you haven't picked up a copy of Gil Hasson's *Mindfulness*, I suggest you do so now. Think of it as a companion book to this one. Hasson's introduction to the concept of Mindfulness explains how it's imperative that individuals practice focusing on the present moment and become aware of the feelings and thoughts that they are experiencing at that instant. Mindfulness prevents you from becoming overwhelmed by your surroundings, or by simply reacting to what is happening around you.

With Mindfulness, you fully tap into your innately human ability to stay connected to the present. It's a quality you, as well as every other human being in the world, possesses already, even if you're not used to accessing it.

Mindfulness is a basic aspect of human nature, but it needs a bit of a boost to be cultivated. This can be done through techniques such as lying down, standing, and walking, meditation. You inculcate Mindfulness by inserting little pauses into your daily life, pauses when you stop thinking about everything in the past and future and remain solely focused on the present moment. You can even combine meditation with activities like sport or yoga in order to become more mindful.

One thing you should keep in mind during meditation – don't spend your time wondering when the benefits are going to kick in. Focus instead on the practice itself. As with so much else in life, it's not about the destination but about the journey. Please also refer to the quote in the very beginning of this book from Fearless Soul (please see under Acknowledgement). Obviously, there are multiple benefits to Mindfulness; it's a key factor in helping you become a more focused and successful person. Mindful people experience lower stress levels and see a spike in their performance. They're more insightful and aware thanks to the practice of observing their own minds. By this time, you might be thinking Mindfulness sounds like just a bunch of hocus-pocus. Or you may worry that you have to be a particularly enlightened person already in order to practice Mindfulness effectively. Neither of those is true. Mindfulness is a practice as familiar and innate to humans as breathing. It's something we already are and already do without even being aware of it. All of us have the capacity to be totally connected to the moment; we don't need to change ourselves for that. Through a few simple practices, we get to tap into a mindset that benefits not just us, but our loved ones, our colleagues, our friends, and neighbors and anyone else we come into contact with.

These practices are scientifically proven. It's not just a bunch of gibberish; it's based on demonstrable evidence. Science and experience both validate its benefits for our overall health, happiness, and success. Best of all, anyone can practice it, especially since it involves qualities that are universally human and doesn't require individuals to go through a transformation of their beliefs. It's a whole way of living that can be incorporated into just about anyone's lives. And in the process, it makes for more innovative individuals with the capacity to formulate resilient and effective responses to seemingly intractable problems in our increasingly uncertain and complicated modern world.

"Drink your tea slowly and reverently, as if it is the axis on which the world earth revolves – slowly, evenly, without rushing toward the future; live the actual moment. Only this moment is life."

-Thich Nhat Hanh

Attain the Beginner's Mind

On page 113 of Mindfulness, Gil talks about the theory of the **Beginner's Mind** - a state of being that encourages you to purge yourself of biases and preconceptions, whether they relate to people, objects or events. Instead, the individual should start on a fresh note, and respond to what is happening in the present rather than to things that they anticipate might occur.

Beginner's mind is an essential aspect of Mindfulness that is as easy to practice as it is difficult to explain. When one is in the beginner's mind state, one is free of expectations, preconceptions, prejudices, and judgments. You throw a fixed point of view out of the window and instead face life with curiosity, amazement, and wonder. The beginner's mind is about looking at things like you're seeing them for the first time ever. It helps you conceive of those things in a new light, bringing a fresh perspective to you. A significant part of building a beginner's mind involves living as if we don't know everything about a situation (which, if you think about it, we never really do.) When we live as if we always have the relevant knowledge, we remain living in the past, unable to have new experiences in the present. There are no discoveries to be made, no surprises, and we remain unable to connect with the present moment.

So how do you go about adopting a beginner's mind?

The first step is to firmly remember that this is actually the natural state of your mind. It's not hard to attain a beginner's mind – you can start to tap into it fairly quickly.

The fact is that a beginner's mind isn't something you achieve. Don't try to open yourself to it; that just creates tension within your own mind and further jars the whole process. No, instead, you need to empty your mind, stripping away all the barriers keeping you from experiencing this state of mind. This is how you return to that natural state; you need to clear all the mental clutter. Here are some ways you could try to empty your mind.

Mindful breathing: Become aware of your very breath. Fixate on the physical process of inhaling and exhaling. It might help to have a locus of awareness on your bodies, such as on your navel or your chest as you inhale and then exhale. You could even focus on the cool rush of air as it enters your nostrils.

What's the point of this? You're trying to centralize all of your focus and attention on one particular action in a single location. In doing so, you draw all of your energy to this central area, which has the effect of quieting the chatter in your mind.

Mindful Observation: For a duration, pick any object and stare at it, without thinking about what that object even is. Rid your mind of the name you associate with that object. Say you're staring at a book. If you didn't know what a book was, or that it was an object meant to be read, how would you visually understand that object? Look at its shape and form, its color and texture. Don't make a judgment regarding what the object is, or what its function is. The longer you do this, the more foreign the item will seem to you until finally, you curiously wonder just what that object is.

This sort of curiosity is a hallmark of the beginner's mind.

Grounding Yourself: Whether you're standing or seated, firmly press your feet into the ground. Focus entirely on the soles of your feet, and how they're in contact with the Earth. Feel a sense of being rooted to the Earth, and stay aware of any sensations your feet may be undergoing. This is an excellent method for calming the mind since it quickly refocuses your attention from your thoughts to a different aspect of your being. Most of our lives, we feel as if there is just too much energy in our minds, and that means we're constantly thinking. But when you shift this attention to your feet, you'll notice a quick change in how this energy operates. You feel a lot more centered as your mind quietens.

Removing How You Identify Yourself: Rid yourself of the way you view yourself. For instance, you might think, "I'm a business graduate, a blonde, an overachiever, a daughter, sister, aunt, mother or father, an international chess player, etc."

Those labels you have are a package deal. They come along with a whole set of beliefs that you associate with that tag. For instance, you may associate your being a mother with a sense of responsibility, or your being a business graduate with being employable. Those labels light up a sort of archetype, triggering you into behaving the way you think that label requires you to behave. The beginner's mind, however, is free of those associations. There are no labels you need to think about. For just a few moments, relinquish the identity you have bequeathed upon yourself.

Remaining Within the Beginner's Mind

As this chapter has noted, the beginner's mind is innate, even though humans tend to lose this basic quality of a conscious mind as they live through the years. A return to this natural state involves installing some new patterns of thought and behavior.

It can help to use the exercises listed above. However, each individual is different, and what works for one person may not work for the next. It's a process of trial and error before you find what's right for you.

Once you've found what fits, use that exercise whenever you need to open your mind to fresh and new possibilities, such as before a project or when you're brainstorming with a team member, or even when you're struggling to make a choice. Remember that your perspective is just that - a perspective, one that is rooted in your unique experiences and the biases that come with it. There could be any number of similarly valid outlooks out there if only you would look for them. Through the beginner's mindset, you open yourself up to these new possibilities and ideas.

If you still have difficulties to see yourself stepping back to where you actually started your life, you may want to use the following picture. Think about life as a giant amusement park. With your birth, you were granted the entrance ticket wristband, and you entered the park full of excitement and curiosity. You couldn't really wait to experience all the new opportunities. You showed no signs of fear for the unknown whatsoever.

It is exactly this feeling that you need to try to preserve, the feeling of a beginner, the capability to see unlimited chances to live a joyful life. The issue faced by you right now is that during all the years and decades of conditioning, you are no longer able to see all the fun-filled bits and pieces of your life. Instead, you have been told that life is about being serious and hard work, right? Here is the solution: The fact that you can't see all your opportunities currently, doesn't mean that they don't exist anymore. It is actually the opposite as you still stand right in the middle of "Disney World." The art is to get rid of your blinkers and get back to a 360-degree view of everything that's reachable for you. Get back to the days when it all began, get back to the beginner's mind.

Faith and Effort

In his book *The Miracle Equation*, Hal Elrod shared the unassuming formula that set him straight on the path to success. It's a straightforward equation: unwavering faith + extraordinary effort = miracles.

Elrod was trying to break the sales record at Cutco when he came up with this formula. The organization would have sales contests where the salesman who made the most sales in 14 days would win. Elrod aimed at making $20K in three back-to-back periods.

However, on the third consecutive period, the 14 days were reduced to simply 10.

Elrod remained unfazed. He simply asked himself what he would have to do in order to reach the goal within this shortened time.

That was how he devised the following intonation: *"I'm committed to maintaining Unwavering Faith that I will sell $20K for push and put forth Extraordinary Effort until I do, no matter what, there is no other option."*

He repeated this to himself until he believed it wholeheartedly. The end result? He made his goal on the very morning of the deadline!

Faith and effort. A combination of the two serves to make you the kind of person who achieves goals by pouring all of your energy into the work, no matter what the results might be. Instead of thinking about how likely it is that you will achieve a goal, you give the goal everything you have until you can no longer do so. In this way, your drive to achieve your goal remains undiminished.

Intention and Emotion

What Hal Elrod explains with his formula "unwavering faith + extraordinary effort = miracles" translates in Dr. Joe Dispenza's groundbreaking book "Becoming Supernatural" into the unbeatable marriage of *clear intention* and *elevated emotion*. It is a three-step plan, simple but very effective. First, you choose a topic of your life that you would like to change – let's say your job. Secondly, you get clarity on how you see your perfect job. Here it is important to get as precise as possible. You might envisage a job that gives you the opportunity to travel the world, gives you the maximum flexibility in terms of when and where to work. It exposes you to a group of inspiring experts on your favorite subject matter. And last but not least, it provides you with more money than your current job. You like that picture? Then write it down on the left side of a blank paper. It is important to visualize yourself having this kind of job already because, in the third step, you go through the list again to add the elevating emotions that come with each of the attributes of your new job. How would this job make you feel? Excited, satisfied, relaxed, energized, …? After going through this three-step process, when you apply what we have learned already about living in the present moment and the unlimited energy field surrounding us this entire time, you combine these techniques to form a powerful concept.

As Dr. Dispenza explained to his son: "*Just hold that symbol in your mind's eye while you radiate that energy (remark from the author: emotion) into the space beyond your body in space.*" This is the essence of the idea that energy flows where attention goes. So, focus your attention, your thoughts, and your feelings on what you really want.

Your Holy Hour

The Miracle Equation is Hal Elrod's second book. His first is *The Miracle Morning,* which he wrote after a battle with cancer in 2016.

In *The Miracle Morning,* Hal outlines a blueprint for personal development that takes place early in the morning. What's great about his practice is that you can modify it for the amount of time you have in the mornings. So, for days that you're super busy and just need to rush out of the house, all you need is to invest six minutes of your time in personal development. Yes, it may be stressful to even think about adding an additional task to your morning routine when you're so harried. But those six minutes can help elevate the remainder of your morning and the rest of the day; they can be life-changing even.

Here's how you spend those six minutes (or longer if you have the time!)

Silence (The First Minute)

When you wake up in the morning, you may be used to a routine of rushing to get showered and dressed before running headlong into your day at breakneck speed. It's a frantic, frenzied way of doing things, and it likely makes you feel overwhelmed and stressed out...right as the day is starting!

Think about how different it would be if you took a different approach to the start of your day. You open your eyes and spend the first minute of your day sitting up in bed in focused, resolute silence. Calmly and peacefully, you remain sitting in a comfortable position and take in deep and slow breaths.

If you're so inclined, you may even say a prayer for guidance or a word of gratitude. It's a meditative minute, one where you prioritize the peace of your mind over the hassle of the day, and you will be the better for it. Stay totally present in the moment as you sit quietly. Relax the muscles of your body and quiet your mind. Let your stresses fall off your back. In this way, you develop a sense of calm and purpose. You set the rhythm for how your day will turn out to be. Choosing to meditate during this period of silence can be especially helpful to people with anxiety. The slow breathing, in combination with the silence and introspection, can do wonders for your troubled and turbulent mind.

Affirmations (The Second Minute)

If you're not in the habit of reading daily affirmations, you should start now. Affirmations are powerful tools in the process of empowerment. These methods help you along the path of self-improvement; they're even proven to rewire how your brain works. Affirmations increase the hormones that make you feel good about yourself, encouraging your brain to break away from negative thoughts and form neurons that create positive thought instead. By affirming your ambitions and dreams out loud, you reassure yourself that your words will transform into reality.

Think up some affirmations that prompt your mind into remembering its unlimited capacity as well as the things that are most important to you. By focusing on your priorities, you will find that your internal motivation grows by leaps and bounds. Reading your affirmations is an excellent reminder of your own capability, and thus it boosts your confidence levels. Think about your purpose in life and what your heart is committed to. Take this minute to visualize your goals and capture the energy necessary to take the relevant actions that will push you closer to the life you want and deserve.

Affirmations are not some sort of mystical, hokey practice. Obviously, it takes hard work and effort to achieve your goals. But people will often tragically downplay the significance of developing a mindset that will drive them to reach those goals. Affirmations can be the final push you need in order to become fully aligned with your goals. The same goes for visualizations, which we'll get to now.

Visualization (The Third Minute)

Do you have a vision board? Remember what you read in the chapter "Formulate a vision" about this great tool. Now we come back to the board (which in the meantime is already hanging at an exposed place in your house) and knit the usage of it into your daily practice.

In the third minute, you look at your vision board and imagine yourself achieving the goals you have set out for yourself. Or if you don't have one yet, you shut your eyes and visualize your goals or even your aspirations for the day.

The sky's the limit in terms of what you visualize. You can try thinking of how you'll feel when you achieve your goals or imagine a day that goes just right for you. This minute of visualization opens your mind to the possibilities squirreled away within the day.

Scribing (The Fourth Minute)

Reach over to your nightstand and pull out the journal you keep in there. Take a few seconds to think, and then write down the things you're grateful for and proud of. Scribble in what you're looking forward to achieving that day. In this process, you empower and inspire yourself, generating confidence in your own abilities to achieve your goals.

According to Elrod, "The simple act of writing down the things I was grateful for lifted my spirits." The science backs up his words; practicing gratitude in our day to day life pushes your brain into feeling happier and can even help you deal with mental health issues like anxiety and depression. Gratitude has a direct correlation with your level of happiness. You may not choose to write out a list of things you're grateful for in the fourth minute. But just the act of thinking about the things that are going well for you in life instead of dwelling on the negatives can shift your mindset remarkably.

Reading (The Fifth Minute)

Pick up your favorite self-help book and spend a minute reading a page. If you're not into self-help books, pick up a novel or a short story and read a page of that instead. In this way, you plant new ideas in your head the first thing in the morning, perhaps even something you can implement in the day to do and feel better. If you prefer videos, choose inspiring, energy lifting ones, for example, from Fearless Soul.

Exercise (The Sixth Minute)

At the last minute, you finally get out of bed and stand up. Then you exercise for a full minute, pumping your heart rate and energizing yourself, so you're alert and able to focus.

Don't you think your quality of life would improve if this was how you started the day? And of course, if you have the time, you can spend more than a minute on each activity.

The Miracle Morning can actually trick you into feeling more motivated and energized bright and early in the day. People who especially enjoy their beauty sleep can find it harder to feel inspired and energetic in the morning. Using this method, however, can help ease the painful process of waking up every day. It might help to set an intention to feel excited and energized before you drop off to sleep as well. It may feel odd to wake up earlier than you usually do at first, but within a few days, you'll find it becomes easier and more natural. It's all about the Compound Effect, which we'll discuss in more detail below in this chapter – small, but effective action, consistently carried out.

Even if you find it hard to stick to a routine, don't worry. It's only natural to fall off the wagon at times; you're only human. Just remain aware that there is a routine you can return to when you're ready for it.

Robin Sharma is also following this rule and encourages everyone to join the so-called "5 o'clock club" and start the day when the rest of the house is still sleeping. I joined the club as well, and I call it my holy hour. Just in case you have difficulties imaging you to get up one hour before you normally get up, the following quote might inspire you to do so.

"It is only when we truly know and understand that we have a limited time on earth – and that we have no way of knowing when our time is up – that we will begin to live each day to the fullest as if it was the only one we had."

-Elisabeth Kubler-Ross

Willpower

From the section about faith and effort above, you would think that willpower is an all-important factor in the process of achieving your goals. And you would be right about that. However, it is imperative that you remember that willpower is a limited source, as Gil Hasson says in *Mindfulness*. You can't keep drawing on it forever; at some point, your stores will be depleted. You're only human, after all. That's why you need to abstain from spreading yourself too thin.

When it comes to willpower, focus on what really matters to you and what is in your control. Let go of goals that you aren't personally invested in – pursuing them will bring you no satisfaction, and that's just going to affect your sense of purpose negatively. You also need to let go of things that aren't in your control. Recognize what external factors are out of your hands and stop pursuing them. You won't be able to bring about any change, and the wasted effort will waste your willpower in the process as well.

Or as Mark Manson explains it in his unique, entertaining manner in the book, *'The subtle art of not giving a f*ck,'* there are only a certain number of fucks you can give during a lifetime, so you better get clarity about what matters to you and hence for what you really want to give a fuck.

It's all about discipline. Figure out which aspects of your life would benefit from you inputting any effort at all, and then pour your heart out in said efforts. Good input means good output, after all.

Letting Go

From Rene Egli's LOLA Principle, we see that the first secret to having better things enter your life is to understand the potential of the let go principle. When you let go of your attachments to what is unnecessary, you create the mental space required to have new and fresh things come into your life: things that will add value to it and help you become a more successful person. Nature serves as a good example. Just like a flowing river that stands for life, letting go and trusting the flow of life means for us to trust in something that is more powerful than we are. As a result, we should stop holding on to things because holding means the opposite of letting go. What you hold on to can't flow/live.

Rene gives a simple example of an archer. An archer takes the bow, he pulls it and takes aim of the object with his arrow. What happens if he remains in that position? You're right, nothing, of course! He needs to let go of the arrow; otherwise, he won't reach his goal.

We can conclude now that let go means life, and holding on to things means standstill or death. So, we better get familiar with the let go principle to get in the flow of life.

For Dr. Wayne Dyer, it was one of his major rules of life. He called it the art to "develop a mind that is open to everything and attached to nothing."

Therefore, paradoxically, the act of letting go actually involves new and improved things coming into your life.

Universal Intelligence

Universal intelligence – the phrase seems to be heavy and loaded, the concept seemingly applicable only to those who have comprehended the mysteries of the universe. And yet, the fact of the matter is that with some practice and given the right mindset, anyone can tap into it. Clichéd as it may sound, what you need in order to access ultimate intelligence is **trust** and **belief**, the acceptance that you are enough to make universal intelligence work.

As Gandhi so famously said, "Be the change you want to see in the world." It's one of those platitudes you come across frequently enough that it loses all meaning. But it's a deeply meaningful statement regardless. The fact is that change starts with yourself, the individual. You can't go through the world expecting other people to change; that's just naïve and will set you up for failure. No, you need to take on the mantle of responsibility and ownership.

Before you implore the people around you to change for the better, you need to change yourself. Take up accountability for what you do; don't try to skip out on the blame for your own actions, or inaction, as the case may be. Instead of finding excuses for everything that goes wrong in your life, and pointing the finger of blame at everything around you, start taking responsibility for your life. As I've mentioned before, you need to get in that driver's seat! You can't stay in the backseat forever, waiting for life to drive you into a tree. The question is now, how do we activate the universal intelligence? The answer is trust. We need to trust in the unlimited power of the universe and the overarching intelligence that supports us to let go of the idea to control everything. It all starts with trust in our own capabilities. Get rid of all limiting beliefs and stop negative self-talk. The more you trust yourself, the more you will trust your environment and, ultimately, the universe. If you distrust life, you cannot expect that life brings you what you really desire.

So, the next time you work on a project, align your energy with the universal intelligence, trust in your capabilities, let go of the idea to be perfect, and step into the river of success. You need to believe it first to see it.

Authenticity

Ultimate intelligence also requires you to be authentic to who you truly are. "Be yourself; everyone else is already taken" said Oscar Wilde, and he was absolutely right about the matter. If you're forever emulating other people, trying to replicate their path to success, you are going to lose sight of yourself and what's important to you.

Everyone has their own unique path to take in life, and you can't achieve the goals that are meaningful to you by following someone else's dreams. All the trying to fit in, the functioning, and self-aligning with society is cutting you off from universal intelligence. When I started my career, I was deeply convinced that I needed to distinguish between my personal and professional lives. In other words, I left my apartment in the morning as Dirk, and the moment I entered the office, I put on my professional mask and played the role of a manager. It took me almost 20 years to understand that by doing so, I unconsciously lived a life resembling that of Dr. Jekyll and Mr. Hyde. But instead of killing people during the night, I killed myself all day long. Since I understood that there is only one Dirk, and since I have clarity about what really matters to me, my life is so much easier as I can simply focus on what is important to me without being distracted by any other fake identity.

With that, I also threw the idea of a work-life balance overboard and ask you to simply maintain a *life balance*. If you can't live while you work, there is something fundamentally going wrong in your life. I suggest you get into a dialogue with yourself, find out what makes your heart sing, and invest your energy to go that direction. Authenticity requires a good understanding of who you actually are. Don't wait and start the journey toward your real identity now.

"To be yourself in a world that is constantly trying to make you something else is the greatest accomplishment."

-Ralph Waldo Emerson

The Compound Effect

The practices outlined in this chapter involve small but effective steps that need to be adopted with persistence and commitment. You can reap gigantic rewards from these little actions that seem almost insignificant when you look at them individually. It's remarkable how these small steps, when strung together on a daily basis, become a powerful chain of consistently carried out actions.

As Robin Sharma says, it's the way we do small things that determines the way we do everything. The attention you pay to the little details of your life spills over into the big things. It's the 24-hour rule. You have 24 hours in a day that you need to give your best (including the hours you spend sleeping.) You have 24 hours to create the life you deserve. A happy life is nothing but 24 hours strung consecutively to a chain. How you spend the first hour of a day will affect the second hour, and so on. It's a cumulative effect. From the very first hour, therefore, you need to be committed to the process of self-improvement and personal development. Never give up and never look back.

Darren Hardy puts it in the following equation:

Small, smart choices + consistency + time = radical difference.

He gives the example of the magic cent. If you were given a choice between taking 3 million dollars in cash now or a single penny that doubles in value every day for 31 days, which would you choose. If you know this example, you also know that the second option is the better choice, as you will have around 10 million dollars after 31 days. The question that arises is why we tend to go for the first option despite knowing the second one is better. Darren concludes: "Because it takes so much longer to see the payoff." Further on in his book "The Compound Effect," he emphasizes that you need to be persistent and very disciplined to get to your goals. It is the capability to stand against headwinds and pull through even when the going gets rough.

In her fascinating book, *The Willpower Instinct,* Kelly McGonigal explains this so-called *delay discounting* phenomenon. The longer you have to wait for a reward, the less it is worth to you. This leads to the fact that we choose immediate satisfaction at the cost of future happiness. McGonigal suggests a simple strategy to trick your subconscious mind: Wait ten minutes! When immediate gratification comes with a mandatory 10 minutes delay, the brain treats it like a future reward.

As a consequence, our reward system is less activated and hence takes away the powerful biological impulse to choose immediate gratification. Moving forward, to support your smart part of the brain, institute a mandatory ten-minute wait for any temptation.

Apart from that, remember that not all storms come to disrupt your life. Some serve the larger purpose of clearing your path to your innermost desires. You know you are on the right track when you have no interest in looking back. Be grateful for all the challenges; they build your character and make you more resilient as you face up to the world. Be grateful for the hard times; they make you appreciate the good times.

Keep It Simple

By now you have read already about quite a number of basic principles in this chapter and before I end this chapter with THE golden rule, and before you start getting confused due to all the potentially new impressions, I would like to introduce to you one of my favorite rules – The rule to keep it simple. You might have heard about it several times before, but this time I would like to ask you to let it sink into your (sub)conscious mind.

How often have you heard that the world is increasingly complex and hard to understand due to globalization, technology, etc.? There is pretty much no conference I appear these days which agenda lacks topics like artificial intelligence, robotics, and block chain technology. Not being tech-savvy, I could easily feel overwhelmed up to the point where I tend to simply give up. When I sense this feeling crawling up in my body, I step back, take a deep breath, and remind myself of what really matters. I don't have to understand all the bits (literally) and pieces about how a certain new invention works. I still wonder, e.g., how my hybrid car manages to seemingly switch from the classic combustion engine to the electric one and back without I even realize it. The fact that I don't know exactly how it works does not prevent me from using it. The point that I want to make is that you need to understand the benefits of new technologies and how it serves the people. Once you have clarity about that and things are put in perspective, they are not so impressive anymore.

Never forget that everything in life, even the most (assumed) complex technology is by the end nothing else but an interpretation of it, to be more precise, your interpretation. In other words, and making a reference here to the power of the free will that we explored earlier in this book, it is purely up to us to interpret our environment the way it serves us best. Magnify the good, inspiring things in your life and let go of the struggles.

The Golden Rule

This chapter focused greatly on tempering your own mind and calming your mental waters in order to achieve personal development and work towards your goals effectively. However, we'll end with the original Golden Rule, the one that our parents work hard to instill within us from childhood: *treat others as you would like to be treated.* This rule deals with your interactions with other people as opposed to how you navigate your mental landscape. It's one of the most important rules you can follow on your path to personal development. While focusing on your own goals is an important part of self-improvement, you can't give yourself tunnel vision in the process.

After all, no man is an island. Remember the principle of giving and receiving; as you sow, so shall you reap. The order is not chosen accidentally; it always starts with giving. If you're overly fixated on yourself to the detriment of your relationships with the people around you, you will become out of balance and isolate yourself. Always be humble and kind in your dealings with people. Kindness cannot help but win.

We have now built respectively rebuilt the second floor of your lighthouse. On your journey to become a responsible, self-driven creator of your life, you got clarity on what basic rules to follow to set the scene. These rules that we have discussed are not exhaustive, and depending on your focus, you might want to add other principles.

But as these ideas have a universal value no matter which background and personal history you carry in your backpack with you, you can apply them in all situations you encounter. These principles serve as a filter and give guidance on how to tackle the daily challenges without feeling overwhelmed. Think about these golden life rules as a toolbox. While you restart your life, it is up to you which tools you want to put into the box so that you always have the correct one at hand. It doesn't help to buy a pre-assembled box with tons of tools that, by the end, you don't need and even confuse you. You only need a few tools but the right ones. What tools are right and which means can serve you the most on your journey toward joy and fulfillment can only be answered by yourself, so choose wisely.

Let me pause here for a few seconds and congratulate you on having pictured your own lighthouse or at least the first part of it. In the meantime, you might have a better understanding of where this book is heading. It always lifts me up when I am working on a project (this book, e.g.), and I see the interim success while I am moving from base camp to base camp on my journey toward the summit. You have achieved the same; the first milestones are done. You can be proud of yourself. In any case, I am proud of you, and I give you the proverbial pat on your shoulder – well done! We move on now to the next floor of your lighthouse and will answer the question about how we turn our foundation and the golden life rules into action and accelerate our lives. No input, no output, but how do we bridge the theory with the practical implementation. The answer is the willingness to change, in other words, to dare and get out of our comfort zone. Believe it or not, the next development step is already waiting for you behind the next door toward the unknown. Enjoy the adventure.

Chapter 5
How to Do It or
Wisdom in Motion

We're on floor three of the lighthouse, well on our way to the top. On the first two floors, we learned the values that would serve as a healthy foundation for our lighthouse. We understood what principles and values were particularly significant to us. We also learned to change our worldview and convictions, delving into the rules of life so we could better understand how to change our perception of the external world.

Change! It can be a difficult concept for people to grapple with. And yet, the funny thing is that we're in a state of change from the moment of our births. We're forced to deal with changes as young children, some of us more so than others. As we grow, some of us learn to welcome change, while others detest it. But no matter what your perception of it is, one thing remains true: change is the only true constant in our life. Before we dive into the magic of change, I would like to share what Steve Jobs wrote when he reached the evening of his life.

"Remembering that I'll be dead soon is the most important tool I've ever encountered to help me make the big choices in life.

Almost everything – all external expectations, all pride, all fear of embarrassment or failure – these things just fall away in the face of death, leaving only what is truly important.

Remembering that you are going to die is the way I know to avoid the trap of thinking you have something to lose. You are already naked. There is no reason not to follow your heart.

No one wants to die. Even people who want to go to heaven don't want to die to get there. And yet, death is the destination we all share. No one has ever escaped it, and that is how it should be because death is very likely the single best invention of life. It's life's change agent. It clears out the old to make way for the new."

Wow! Whenever I read through this piece, I need a few seconds to digest what it means and let it sink in. If these words have a similar impact on you, feel free to pause and reflect on it for a while before you continue reading. So why do people resist change? Maybe it's because change always has some perceived fear or risk associated with it. Even when we wish to change, we have an awful time of it following through. Just think of the smoker who's trying to quit or the workaholic who's trying to stop biting off more than they can chew. It's only too common to react to change with doubt, fear, and other negative emotions.

There are certain habits that we find harder to change than others. For instance, the habits we get accustomed to during stressful times are hard to get rid of. Let's say you developed a habit of chewing your fingernails during a difficult time in your life. This habit is now a part of the fight-flight-or-freeze response that's activated whenever you're under stress – a response that's hardwired into your brain.

Obviously, that makes for a habit that needs time and effort to resolve. Similarly, it's also hard to get rid of habits like substance addiction, since these are linked to chemical changes in your brain. Finally, there are habits that you're not totally motivated to transform. You're not starting with a full deck when you try to change these habits; from the very outset, you're low on emotional motivation.

So just what do we do about this difficult concept of change? How do we embrace this inevitability instead of resisting it? How do we welcome positive changes in our lives without becoming completely overwhelmed by them?

That's what the third floor of the lighthouse is all about.

Let's first talk about structuring your perception towards a goal to make it more change-friendly.

Your Perception of a Change You Want to Make

There is no bigger mental block to change than your own perception of it. Let's say that you've been smoking for ten years. You've always had a nagging feeling at the back of your mind that you should quit, but the habit's just too ingrained. It brings you too much comfort.

It's a stress-reliever. By this point in time, you reach out for a cigarette without even thinking about it. But you've also been worried about the effects it has had on your health for a long time. You've noticed you've been coughing a lot more than you used to, and you're short of breath after just a minute of exercise. Clearly, you need to make a change if you want to live a long, healthy life.

So you decide to quit. It's what you're meant to do, isn't it? But you view this decision with extreme irritation. If you quit smoking, you're essentially taking away a means of coping with stress and the pressures of your life. You're being forced to stop something that's pleasurable to you, and replace it with withdrawal symptoms and cravings.

No wonder you view it as a negative change. How are you going to follow through with this decision when the very thought of it makes you angry?

So what do you do?

Well, first of all, you need to acknowledge this change. Evaluate the reasons you've made this decision at all. What made you decide to quit smoking? Was your doctor nagging at you? Was it your family? Did you make the decision because you felt you were obligated to do so, or because you're truly ready to make a positive change?

That's the important detail that makes all the difference.

You can't make a real change to please other people or out of a sense of obligation. Any changes you make have to be for your own sake.

The first and most important step is to create a **sense of urgency**. The part in your life that you don't like (anymore) and hence you would like to change has to be something that is either extremely disturbing (e.g., smoking), or it is a lack, a vacuum, a skill set that you dream of already for a long time (e.g., learn to play the guitar). To get there, you have to have an honest and sometimes painful discussion with yourself. Only if the topic is really important for you, and you want to have it changed from the bottom of your heart, you are ready for the next step.

"If you truly want to get something done, you will find a way. If you don't, you will find an excuse."

-Jim Rohn

Let's take a look at the quitting smoking example again. You need to envision the change as one that will bring about positive changes in your life, and not just take a source of enjoyment away from it. But to do so, you need to first make peace with the situation you want to change. Breathe in, breathe out, and reflect on the situation that you want to change. Try to put it in perspective and ask yourself, e.g., the following questions.

What does it actually mean now, and in 5 years from now on? What's the worst that could happen? What's good about it, and what can I learn from it? How can I use it? What exactly did I screw up, and what was my role in it. Simply look at yourself as an outside spectator without any judgment. That's the next step: **acknowledge the current situation**. Acknowledge it and let go of any resentments or regrets.

"Resentment is like drinking poison and waiting for it to kill your enemy."

-Nelson Mandela

Step three is **accepting the situation** as it unfolds.

It needs some courage to look into the mirror and admit that you are fully responsible for the current situation. If you still think it happened accidentally or even start finding excuses and point the finger to others, you might want to read the chapter about the law of attraction again. Life, means moving out of your comfort zone, is about responsibility and the trust that it had to happen this way to get the opportunity to grow personally, a test for your character. Accepting is an exercise between you and yourself, not between you and society. So, stop thinking about the past (it is done anyhow) and other people, stop your regrets and promise yourself to learn from it and to grow. Back to the cigarettes, you know this goal of yours will bring about some much-desired health benefits to your life. But you also know that there will be some negative side effects as well: you'll crave cigarettes badly, go through withdrawal symptoms, have difficulty focusing on tasks and managing stress, and have to deal with increased irritability. Don't shy away from these side effects or close your eyes to their presence. Accept reality for what it is; those negative effects are well and present, and you need to learn to manage them. If you don't give these effects their due recognition, how will you develop the mental tools to deal with them?

Step four is **visualizing your goal**. You remember the concept of visualization from the last chapter. Visualization techniques have been proven to help you achieve your desired outcomes. By routinely visualizing your goal, you prompt your brain to gather the mental resources it needs to achieve it. It also motivates you to take the necessary actions to achieve these dreams. You can visualize your goal in your mind, or you can make a vision board to help you in this activity. Finally, you need to **take action**. For this, you need to figure out what course of action will help you achieve your goal. In the smoking example, will it help you to use nicotine patches? Would it be useful to make an appointment with a hypnotherapist, or to keep a pack of lollipops so you can stick one in your mouth whenever you feel the cravings? You need to outline your plan of action clearly. Even if you don't stick to this plan of action as consequently as you would like, you know it's there for you to return to.

Above all, remember the compound effect. We've talked about this in earlier chapters. Keep at a series of small habits with consistency, and these will eventually lead to larger, compound results. The fact of the matter is that effective changes aren't the ones made overnight, but small, incremental ones that lead to long-lasting outcomes.

Change through Mindfulness

We've talked a lot about practicing mindfulness, and it comes into handy here as well.

Here's a quote from Jon Kabat-Zinn, a forerunner in the field of mindfulness, about how the practice can be used to facilitate change: "Mindfulness can be thought of as moment-to-moment, non- judgmental awareness, cultivated by paying attention in a specific way, that is, in the present moment, and as non-reactively, as non-judgmentally, and as openheartedly as possible. ... For mindfulness is none other than the capacity we all already have to know what is actually happening as it is happening."

That's what mindfulness is all about: awareness. Not only does it make you more aware of your surroundings, but it also makes you more conscious of your very mind. You become attentive to your mind's own habits and inclinations. In the process, you understand how to change your mind for the better, so it becomes a valuable tool in your quest for a particular change. By developing an awareness of your own mental habits, you pave the way to changing them, so they serve you, not the other way around.

As we've discussed before, you develop mindfulness through activities that help you gain awareness of the moment you're living through. These include meditation, yoga, long walks through nature and the arts: it's anything that helps you appreciate where you are right now. Why is mindfulness such a natural part of bringing about real change? It's all down to how it strengthens your awareness of your own mind. When you're aware of your mind, you can observe for yourself the changes that need to be made. You can't change something that's without the scope of your awareness, after all. This kind of mental awareness is exactly what we need to cut through the routine of our habits and behavior, allowing us to make more conscious choices in our lives. Not only do you become more aware of your conscious behaviors, but you also take stock of behaviors you weren't all that mindful of before, such as minute shifts in your impulses and emotions.

For someone looking to make changes in their life, this kind of awareness has more value than can be expressed. Instead of just springing into action every time we have a thought, it helps us become aware of the thought, and then the reasons behind that thought. This helps you make choices that are more informed by your understanding of the situation.

As we said, change is inevitable. You may not be able to stop it, but you can certainly learn to manage the uncertainty and anxiety you feel. You can learn to accept it even as you gain awareness of both the situation and your own mental and emotional responses to it.

Here's how you use mindfulness to guide you along the process of change. First of all, accept the inevitability of the change. It's going to happen whether you like it or not. Willingly accept the change, and you save yourself a world of pain. Reinforce the fact that change is coming, and you'll be able to adapt to change without having to face a whole lot of internal resistance.

Secondly, take account of your own feelings and thoughts regarding change. You could see it as either good or bad, depending on your outlook. You already have a set of automatic responses built in your system, and these greatly affect your position on change. If you're not aware of these responses, you'll just keep having them without quite understanding why.

By observing your thoughts, you can make the decision to stay attached to them, or lose them. You need to totally understand how you currently feel about the change you are experiencing: is it excitement that you're feeling or hesitancy? Maybe it's anger, fear, anxiety, or a combination of any of these. Your feelings could even conflict with each other. That's where it helps to take some time to quietly reflect on the change. Think about what is going through your mind and what you're feeling. You can even write your emotions down to sort them out. Thirdly, think about how the change impacts you. The effect could be large or small. By anticipating the effects of the change, you will be able to manage your expectations and therefore adapt to the situation with more efficacy. In this stage, you'll count both the positive and negative ways the change will affect you. Change is often linked to opportunity, which is why it can help you to have a different perspective on the matter. Even negative changes will often have some positive outcomes.

Fourthly, try to adapt to the change. The more flexibility you exhibit here, the easier you will find it to get through the change. Let go of beliefs that limit you and embrace the potential you have for personal growth and development. Think about how you can change yourself or your life in order to balance the situation that you are currently in.

Fifthly, make conscious decisions. Break down the way forward into small chunks of easily manageable goals. This will help you recognize any obstacles in your way, and let you figure out the appropriate solutions to overcome them. Think through these solutions, so you know how likely they are to succeed. If you want to climb the Mount Everest, you do it from base camp to base camp, right?

Sixthly, meditate. Meditate whenever you feel overwhelmed; it will help you get over the feeling and find some acceptance and peace of mind.

Creating a Long Term Strategy for Change

When someone seeks," said Siddhartha, "then it easily happens that his eyes see only the thing that he seeks, and he is able to find nothing, to take in nothing because he always thinks only about the thing he is seeking, because he has one goal, because he is obsessed with his goal. Seeking means: having a goal. But finding means: being free, being open, having no goal."

-Hermann Hesse

Real and lasting change comes in small incremental steps. That means that it's vital to plan out a long-term strategy that breaks your larger goals down. For instance, you can break a long-term goal (buying a house, for instance) down to one-year plans (make a down payment in the next two years), which are further broken down to four quarters (making a certain amount of money every quarter). One quarter equals three months.

Planning is an all-important part of success. That's for three reasons:

Planning gives an individual clarity about their goals.

Clarity is probably the most important basis for individual success. If you don't know where you want to be in 3, 6, or 12 months from now on, you are logically only a victim of your circumstances. Hence, you tend to follow the direction forced upon you by others. It takes a bit of discipline to break the habit of receiving the goals from other people, e.g., from your friend (let´s go to the cinema), from your boss (finalize the report by tomorrow EOB) or your parents (study law at the XYZ university).

Instead, you should block some time to reflect, install the holy hour as I call it. Take a blank piece of paper and write down everything that pops up in your mind that makes you feel good. Dare to think without any limits (time, money, intelligence…). What is it that you dream of? Being an actor? Playing in a band? Going on an off-road trip to Mongolia? Designing fashion? Writing a book (obviously one of my goals in 2019/2020), getting in good shape…?

Simply collect all these ideas, no matter how small or big. You can call it your dream book. Once the collection is done, you put priorities next to your goals. Take the first two or three goals and put them on a separate piece of paper and note down how it would make you feel having accomplished your vision. Do as if you have already achieved your dreams and surf the law-of-attraction wave.

Planning helps you figure out how to create a structure for achieving your specific goal. You can write out your goals and organize them into the category of either short-term or long-term goals, and it will help you develop a roadmap.

When you sit down and think about how you're going to achieve a particular goal, it helps you to break the ultimate goal in smaller milestones that are easier to reach. Instead of getting frustrated when looking at the summit of Mount Everest, get focused on walking from base camp to base camp. Never forget about the compound effect. It is not the big one-off achievement that will make you feel fulfilled. It is the multiple, small but effective, and consistently carried out actions that produce a long-term effect of well-being.

Careful planning prepares you for the reality of your goals. It helps you identify the tools you need to add to your toolbox, the means that will help you to reach your goals. You want to learn a new language, find a teacher, a language school, or an online course. Book a trip to the respective country where you will be exposed to native speakers.

Always have in mind, clarity is key. The clearer your goals in every single detail, the more likely it is that you will live your dream.

Planning forces you to define your goals within a specific timeframe

One of the biggest blocks that keep people from achieving their goals is the lack of a timeframe. This means that they keep pushing their goals off to another day. "I'll start my exercise regimen tomorrow." "I'll start playing the guitar when I have time."

A good plan, however, includes a very specific timeline for your course of action. By giving yourself a restriction, you develop a greater sense of urgency about your goal; it becomes something you prioritize, not the last thing on your mind. This helps to sharpen your mind, focus on what really matters, and challenges your discipline. Timing, though, is a sensitive topic when planning your life, and it comes with a caveat. We know in the meantime about the beauty of the law of attraction and the mechanics behind this universal principle. In other words, we can trust that we have a powerful companion on our way towards reaching the desired outcomes – yes, we will finally win the jackpot. BUT, the law of attraction doesn't commit to any deadline or ultimate day of achievement. So, please don't get frustrated when a specific goal is not reached after the 90 days you gave yourself for accomplishment. Apply the let go principle and trust the universe; it is on its way!

It enables you to think about what you aspire to achieve

Planning gives you a clearer perspective of what is important to you and what you hope to achieve. When you formulate your goals and develop a roadmap, you focus on the things you wish to accomplish. Planning keeps you from wasting time on what is not important to you; it helps you prioritize your affairs and devote time to them in accordance with their importance. A plan is working like a filter that you put in front of you. Things that are coming along your way that are not contributing to reaching your goal, and hence would cause you to get distracted and lose focus, will not pass the filter. It is the function of a good plan to prevent you from dealing with irrelevant information and boost your way to success with supportive relationships, relevant data, and good energy.

Now you have a plan, but as the saying goes, even a journey of 20,000 miles starts with the first step. How to get into the starting blocks?

The 5 Second Rule

You have a goal, and you have a plan – well done! Now it is the first day of getting into the steps and start riding the horse, based on experience, the first cut is the deepest. So, how to get started?

The 5 Second Rule is a mental technique utilized by writer Mel Robbins. According to her, everyone knows exactly what they have to do to achieve what they want. You can easily figure out the steps involved in achieving your dreams from just a Google search. So, why don't you do it? Well, Mel says it's because it's never enough to simply know what you do. There's no switch you can press in your brain to just get up and do it. No, you have to create a strong foundation in order to take action; first, we have to overcome our own emotions and blocks. In a nutshell, if you don't want to do something, you won't do it. It's not enough to know what to do, or why you need to do it. You need something else to launch you into action. Remember, you are now on your way to leave your comfort zone.

You will do something new that you haven't done so far to achieve something that you haven't achieved so far. So, this is the theory. Let's see how your body reacts. Your subconscious mind will throw you off in a split second by giving at least ten reasons why you should not go that way. This is a natural reaction that, with the best intentions, tries to protect you from the unknown – the danger. This mechanism is already 50,000 years old and ensured that we are still on planet earth while Mr. Saber-toothed Tiger quit a long time ago.

In other words, we need to trick our own disaster recovery program and go beyond the invisible line of safety. That's where the 5 Second Rule comes in. It goes like that: if you feel the instinct to act on a goal, move to accomplish it within five seconds before your brain subconsciously axes your idea. We all know this feeling; for once, we want to get up earlier than usual to do some exercise before work. We set our alarms at 5:30 am, and are fully committed and highly motivated the night before. However, the moment the alarm goes off a few hours later, what do we do? Exactly! Our commitment heads of on vacation, our motivation has fallen asleep, and the snooze button suddenly becomes our best friend.

Here is the antidote: The count-down, or as Mel Robbins would call it, *"The 5-second rule."* The moment the alarm goes off, you immediately count down from five, and by the time you hit one, you find yourself already standing next to your bed, wondering what happened.

Why is that working? The moment you start counting down, you trick your subconscious mind. While counting down and getting focussed on "the moment of truth" your subconscious mind cannot throw any distracting thoughts to you (e.g., it's too early for exercising, only 5 minutes, I can start tomorrow, I need my beauty sleep, etc.) that would block you from getting up. The reason behind this is that your conscious mind is in control while counting. Hence, the subconscious mind can't intervene. Very simple, but equally effective. With the 5 Second Rule, you effectively switch gears in your brain, so it works with every change you want to establish in your life. Use this rule to trigger yourself into action instead of procrastination.

Using Meditation in Your Planning

Meditation and mindfulness guru, Dr. Joe Dispenza, says something similar to what Mel Robbins experienced. Probably, you are completely prepared and ready to act in a certain way when it comes to translating your vision into action. What keeps us from changing then? Our emotions and feelings. These emotions and feelings arise from our cumulative experiences. They're how your brain remembers past events. And if these emotions become part of how you remember experiences in your long-term memory, they become part of how you approach new experiences as well.

That's the rub. We use our feelings and emotions to determine our path going forward. And yet, they are a reflection of the past. If we are to change, we need to leave our former ways of thinking, feeling, and acting behind. So, we have a new outlook as we move into the future. Already simply thinking about it makes you feel uncomfortable?

Congratulations, it means you are on the right track. And never forget:

"If you always do what you've always done, You'll always get what you've always got."

-Henry Ford

How do we think about change? Well, we need to learn to free our minds from external stimuli and learn that we already have everything we need inside of us. The challenge is to stop seeking answers in our environment, stop comparing and copying, end to play a role that is imposed on us by society. Instead, slow down, reflect, breathe in and out, and listen to our natural needs.

It also means spending more time in the presence. Have you ever realized that we spend most of the time producing thoughts triggered by our past? Thoughts and hence feelings about regrets, anger, or denial have their roots in our childhood. Obviously, it is tough to get focused on the here and now when carrying a backpack stuffed with unprocessed events that had a highly emotional impact. On the other hand, the world is turning faster and faster, and hence changes kick in much more frequently than we were used to.

As a consequence, predictability decreases, and insecurity increases. In this kind of a situation, our subconscious mind is working well and switches back the caveman mode. Even the smallest potential threat will be seen through a magnifier glass. You know the feeling when there is already enough work on your desk that makes you feel overwhelmed, and then your boss comes around the corner and asks you to do something on top? Now your brain switches to flight-or-fight mode, it releases the stress hormone cortisol, and the rest is a biological chain reaction in your body. Result: you are afraid of what's waiting for you around the next corner, and you are full of doubts about how to deal with all that.

So, how to recalibrate your mind to start enjoying the present time? It's a skill that can be trained, a skill with the capacity to break usual patterns of thinking and prepare you for the future. One way to develop this skill is through meditation. Reserving the time on a daily basis to stop the autopilot and hence break the program that is running in the back of your brain will effectively help you to calm your restless mind. It will help you think of the behaviors you want to change and figure out new ways of doing so.

"Meditating is also a means for you to move beyond your analytical mind so that you can access your subconscious mind. That's crucial since the subconscious is where all your bad habits and behaviors that you want to change reside."

-Dr. Joe Dispenza

Breaking Bad (Habits)

The first step to breaking a bad habit is to become aware of it. The problem with bad habits is that they're so much a part of our routine that we enact them without even thinking about it. One way you can reflect on your habits and their impact on your life is through journaling.

Once you know there's a habit you want to change or adapt (e.g., stop eating sweets in front of the TV), write down that change in your journal as a goal you want to achieve. Then list the action steps (e.g., stop buying sweets and store them at home to be ready for the next TV-evening-excess) you take routinely in order to break out of that habit or to get into the new (better) one. Identify what triggers your bad habits. Maybe you tend to spend too much when you go to a particular outlet. Maybe you crave a cigarette more when you're around certain people you dislike. Note down in your journal when your bad habits tend to occur, and then figure out how to alter the situation, so they don't get triggered.

Use your journal to outline and create a plan that helps you avoid triggers and act on behaviors that you want to adopt. Surround yourself with people who you adore because of certain behaviors (men of sports, people who like to read and write, dancers or singers, adventurers…). You should spend much more time with people that live by example, people that already sit in the driver seat of their lives. It is the leader of the pack that can teach you lessons, not a bunch of followers.

Remember, change is incremental. It takes a lot of time. Little changes you make add up over time; you need to keep at it. Maybe you can use your journal to document small successes. Give yourself a pat on the back for these; celebrating your successes motivates you to remain persistent.

"5 small wins a day adds up to 1825 wins in 12 months. Consistency breeds mastery!"

-Robin Sharma

Keep the compound effect in mind at all times. This is the tactic of winning large rewards from a series of small, effective actions that seem insignificant on their own. Darren Hardy outlines this in his book, *The Compound Effect*. In this, he talks about how success is doing a few things really well 5000 times over. The key to significant results is persistence and consistency. Success is the logical consequence when you string a series of tiny action points to a beautiful string over time.

Too much of our time is wasted thinking about big choices when the fact of the matter is that the small ones are the ones that disrupt our course. Your small decisions and actions are what bring about change in your life.

Track your progress, behavior, and setbacks. Make changes in your life within a given timeframe. Then, at the end of that timeframe, measure the results you see and make small course corrections to improve your performance. Be the captain of your ship, and always be on the lookout for behaviors that are crawling up intending to become (bad) habits.

Overcoming Limiting Beliefs

You know you want to achieve a goal, and you know how to do it too. So, why don't you do it? Oftentimes, our own beliefs about ourselves and our capacity to create a picture of our best self limit us. We don't believe ourselves to be capable of achieving our goals. The issue is that this happens subconsciously most of the time.

In order to overcome these limiting beliefs, you first have to become aware of them. Typical examples are: I don't have enough time, I am not clever enough, the challenge is simply too big, and so on. In your journal, write your five biggest limiting beliefs. Number them according to how ingrained each belief is.

Then draw these numbers on five objects, such as on five small stones that you can easily carry with you. Alternatively, of course, you can write the numbers down on different strips of paper and carry them around with you. Now go for a walk in the woods or stroll along a nice beach. Every now and then, pull out one of the stones that represent your limiting beliefs and drop them. These signify letting them go. That's a key concept of mindfulness: the letting go principle. We tend to strongly fixate on certain ideas and beliefs, and we cling to them tightly. When we want to achieve something, we reach out for it, but our pre-existing ideas anchor us and keep us from our goals. Letting go of those ideas frees you from that imprisoning belief system.

On your way back from the woods or the beach, you will feel lighter and freer. You have let go of the physical manifestations of your limiting beliefs, and in the process, you have made space for something new. On another piece of paper, write down the goals you would like to accomplish. Collect five other items that represent your new, limitless beliefs, and carry these around instead of the stones that were weighing you down earlier. I am carrying with me, e.g., a stone with a smiley to remind me not to take myself too seriously.

How to embrace constant change in a frantic world

I would like to refer at this point to the principle of adaptation as it is outlined in Mike Rother's book: *The*

Toyota Kata Practice Guide. The basis for this approach is the assumption that the future is no longer predictable. Instead, constant change is the new, overarching paradigm. So, how can we get prepared for instability and constantly changing environmental conditions?

> *"There are perhaps only three things we can and need to know with certainty: Where we are. Where we want to be, and by what MEANS we should maneuver the unclear territory between here and there. And the rest is supposed to be somewhat unclear because we cannot see into the future! The way from where we are to where we want to be next is a gray zone full of unforeseeable obstacles, problems, and issues that we can only discover along the way. The best we can do is to know the approach and the means we can utilize for dealing with the unclear path to a new desired condition, not what the content and steps of our actions – the solution – will be."*
>
> **-Excerpt from Toyota Kata, Mike Rother**

Adapting to change is a difficult process if you attempt to bring it about all at once. There is only one way to adapt yourself to change in a long-lasting way, and that's by consistently and continuously implementing your response to the change.

The Toyota Kata Practice Guide by Mike Rother outlines the Toyota Kata: a focused and structured approach to developing continuous improvement and learning. While the book was written from a management perspective, the Toyota Kata can easily be applied to personal adaptation to change as well. It involves implementing continuous learning and improvement into your very routine. These changed habits and routines then help endeavor to achieve your vision.

The principle idea behind the Kata approach is scientific thinking. Scientific thinking is the antidote to our natural intention to jump to a conclusion without having enough data available to make an informed decision. Making a fast decision is an "energy-saving, better-safe-than-sorry approach that's beneficial when a fast reaction is more valuable than deep understanding." Fifty thousand years ago, this approach made perfect sense when you heard a strange noise behind a bush. The subconscious mind immediately created a worst-case scenario (the saber-toothed tiger!), and an artificial stress situation was created to kick-off the fight-or-flight reaction. Result? Survival! Scientific thinking would have been the wrong choice. Imagine Einstein asking his family members in a similar situation: "Hey, I wonder what that is." Result? Extinction! Today, there are less immediate threats around us. Instead, the saber-toothed tiger was replaced by a constantly changing environment, relationships, and technology. In such an environment, it is helpful to stop on a regular basis and do proper research to collect what is necessary to decide on the next step forward. Or, as Mike Rother puts it: "Scientific thinking is the best way we have to avoid being fooled by our perceptions."

He describes two major Kata, which means structured routines or a way of improving, in his book. These are the Improvement Kata and the Coaching Kata, both of which place high importance on learning.

The **Improvement Kata** forms the very core of the Toyota Kata. This is what develops the methods habits of continuous improvement. It guides the learners through a learning-focused process that improves their working methods. There are four steps to this process.

The first step is to understand the direction we desire to go in. It's important to first theorize about what you think is important, and how you will go about making the relevant improvement. Without this, you can easily lose sight of your purpose, and therefore find it harder to remain motivated. With a clear understanding of the direction you want to take, you develop a sense of purpose about the process of improvement. Envision what you need to do to achieve your goal and focus on the process instead of the outcome.

The second step is to have a firm grasp of the current condition. You need to fully comprehend the reality of where you are at the present time. Develop a clearer picture of what you're doing right now and how your processes work. You can create a quick flowchart of the steps involved in the process. Then outline how these processes lead to particular outcomes, the results of your current process.

The third step is establishing the next conditions for your target. You know what direction you want to head in, and are aware of your present conditions. Now, you need to describe your preferred state in the future. Your new target condition will outline the way your process needs to work in order to reach your desired state. Again, this is not focused on the outcome, but the process itself. Think of the target condition as a hypothesis that you need to prove your theory of improvement. Your target condition should also have a specific timeframe, to motivate you and create a sense of urgency.

The fourth step is a Plan-Do-Check-Act or PDCA cycle towards the target conditions. The PDCA cycles are little experiments designed to eliminate one obstacle in your way at a time. This helps you learn just how your processes work, and thus, you use your learning to adjust your theory. By following the Development Kata, you experiment with the meta-skills that define the how-to, not the what-to.

The second Toyota Kata is the **Coaching Kata**. This complements the Improvement Kata, allowing you to learn and improve, and guiding you in the right direction. Primarily, the Coaching Kata supports the Improvement Kata's fourth step. It usually applies to the leaders in an organization, who will take on a supporting and coaching role with their teams.

However, it can also apply to your personal goals. Is there someone you look up to? Ask them to be your coach or mentor, and have them keep an eye on your progress. Ask them for help when you stumble across a roadblock, or when you need guidance moving forward. Combined, these Katas will help you develop routines that are focused on learning and improvement, even as you navigate the uncharted territories of change and new goals. The Toyota Kata offers in the first place a solution for the corporate world. But even the biggest corporate organization on this planet is by the end nothing else but a group of people. As such, we can also apply the Kata approach to solve individual challenges or:

"Any organization's competitiveness, ability to adapt and culture arise from the routines and habits by which the people in the organization conduct themselves every day. It is an issue of human behavior."

-Mike Rother

At the end of this chapter, we have learned how to leverage our strong foundation and the golden life rules from the previous chapter. We have added tools that will support us on how to turn theoretical knowledge into practical application, or as it´s referred to in the subtitle of this book – wisdom in motion.

The third floor of our lighthouse is ready, so let´s move on to the ultimate experience of shining a light for others.

Chapter 6
Shine a Light for Others

"I am a giant,

Stand up on my shoulders,

Tell me what you see."

This lyric from Calvin Harris and Rag 'n' Bone Man's collaborative single *Giant* alludes to Isaac Newton's famous phrase 'Standing on the shoulders of giants.' Newton meant that his achievements in the field of science were not a credit to him alone; his contributions had been helped by those who had preceded him.

Within the context of *Giant*, the narrator is inviting others to stand on his shoulders and see beyond the horizon, beyond the limited beliefs. Standing on someone's shoulders helps to get rid of the blinkers and allows a full view of the unlimited opportunities life offers us.

That's what a lighthouse does.

We're now on the final floor of the lighthouse we've been building. We're at the very top.

Let's talk about the function of a lighthouse.

A lighthouse is a beacon of light standing tall amidst the darkness, a constant guide for people even when they feel at sea.

We built our lighthouse out of a foundation of values and erected its structure based on our worldview and our approach to change. Thus, as we walked up the stairs, we reached the room that emanates a guiding light to others in our lives.

That's the role that you can let your values play in your life. By making sure they're a rock-solid structure that holds up your decisions in life, you become a guiding light for other people to follow.

It takes a lot of focus and energy to negotiate the circumstances of your life and to navigate its ups and downs. Sometimes, it seems completely overwhelming to just survive the choppy seas without getting wrecked on the rocks.

That's where the lighthouse comes in.

Its guiding light is visible in every single weather condition, and as such, reliably provides us with direction and a sense of stability. It leads the way forward when everything is well, and it's what we need when there's a storm blowing. Instead of being pushed around by stormy seas and crashing on rocks, you get to chart your own path in life.

It's time to reclaim our own special light and shine it for all the world to see, so those who are drifting can find their own way. It's time to be the giants other people can stand on.

The Worth of Service

Here's a difficult question you should think about for a few minutes:

How much of your life have you spent either in service yourself or thinking of yourself?

The answer tends to be quite similar for most people. Human beings are inherently selfish animals, after all. It's natural for us to think about ourselves first, it's our own experiences we feel the deepest connection to. Even when we're not thinking about ourselves, we're serving ourselves. We feed and clothe our bodies for ourselves. We sleep for ourselves. And in the process, we become disconnected from the wider world at large.

This disconnect ends up costing us. No man is an island. We all need each other, and as such, we all need to be in constant service to each other. It may not come naturally to all of us to be of service to other people, but it is vital that we try.

Let's see what motivational speaker and Internet personality Jay Shetty has to say on the topic. His metaphor for being of service to others is: *planting trees under whose shades you won't sit.*

Jay Shetty talks of the time he met a monk during a transformative phase in his life. He had lost two friends, one to a car accident and the other to drugs and violence. The tragedy forced him to reevaluate his worldview. His meeting with the monk was the final piece that shifted his perspective. As he was talking to the monk, Jay, found out that the man had given up opportunities at both Microsoft and Google in order to be a monk instead.

It dumbfounded Jay. After all, who gives up a (materially) successful life like that to live in such an ascetic fashion? The very idea seemed antithetical to the life Jay and his friends were pursuing. And yet, the monk seemed to have found happiness in his life, a quality that was still elusive to the people Jay had met before.

Then the monk said something that caused Jay to have a change of heart about how to live his life.

The monk said that we need to plant trees under whose shades we do not sit. These trees are not for our benefit; they are planted solely for other people.

Those words deeply resonated with Jay. That idea of selfless sacrifice permeated his entire being.

You can feel the thrill he felt, too, because the truth of the matter is that there is no greater ideal than sacrificing your own joys for the betterment of other people. Even if you're not a religious person, there is an element of spirituality and wholesomeness about it that has the power to change your life totally.

As Jay notes, many people with successful careers and beautiful spouses still remain dissatisfied with their lot in life, as if there's a void that hasn't been filled. There's a lack of purpose and fulfillment in these lives, and no matter how hard they try to bridge the gap using material riches, somehow, it never works out.

It is strange then that this is still the model of life most people aspire to. You look at influencers on Instagram or famous and wealthy celebrities, and you think that they've got it all. They've got it made. And they sell their apparent happiness well enough that you think this is what you need to have in order to be happy yourself. But the truth is that unless you fill that void with something meaningful and purposeful, you're going to remain dissatisfied and unfulfilled.

That's where being of service comes in. The more you help the people around you, the more fulfilled and worthy you will feel.

I case you still need some scientific proof that being of service is, by the end, a selfish thing to do, as you serve yourself by helping others. Here it is. Let's look at what happens inside your body when being of service. Let's say you walk down the street, a guy stumbles in front of you, and all his belongings are spread over the sidewalk. Instead of continuing to walk, you decide to give him a helping hand despite the fact you might get too late for your appointment. There is a magic hormone called oxytocin that is released by your body in moments like that, moments when you put aside your own needs and instead give your valuable time to others. At that moment, you feel fulfilled and get the impression that you have contributed to something bigger than yourself. That is the reason why oxytocin is also called the 'bond hormone,' it is like natural glue for our society. And by the way, even people that are only watching the scene will get a little zip of oxytocin released in their bodies.

So we are social animals that are programmed to help each other. But to do so, you need to be ready for it, ready in terms of knowing who you are and what really matters to you. It is like sitting in a plane and listening to the safety instructions. In case the cabin pressure drops, who is it that you put the oxygen mask on first? Right! It is you first, and then you are asked to take care of the other passengers, or your kids. So, let's talk about responsibility.

Taking Responsibility for Your Own Life

Before you can be responsible for other people, you first have to take responsibility for your own life.

"I'm starting with the man in the mirror I'm asking him to change his ways...."

-Michael Jackson, Man in the Mirror

Too often, we will blame our failures and hang-ups on extenuating circumstances. And yes, that's fair to a great extent. The world is a difficult place to live in. Plenty of factors are absolutely out of our control, and at times, it can feel as if there's nothing you can influence to your advantage.

Except that's not quite true. As someone who has been reading this book, you know that change is possible and within your grasp.

You need to identify the factors you cannot influence and then let go of any illusion of control you might have regarding them.

Once you have done that, you are left with what you can control. This is what you can manipulate in order to improve your lot, and have a happier, healthier, more stimulating life. But for that, you need to take responsibility for those factors. You need to be responsible for your goals.

Taking responsibility for your goals is something you need to do on a daily basis. As we've discussed before, change comes in incremental steps; you cannot rush this. Use the steps outlined in earlier chapters and do so regularly; you will eventually realize the goals you have set for yourself.

As you mature in your spiritual journey, you will naturally experience a shift in your priorities and your perspective. You stop focusing all your attention on yourself and become less self-centered. With the passage of time, you'll even find that the lines blur between your own needs and the needs of others, meaning your own happiness becomes linked to that of others.'

There's a reason mystics and spiritual gurus leave the material world behind to live a life of service. They don't find it spiritually fulfilling to only live for themselves anymore, as we can see from the example of the monk that Jay Shetty met. The purpose of their lives undergoes a transformation; no longer is their sole aim to satisfy their own desires, but to be of benefit to humanity.

That said, it's important to remember one thing. Being of service does not mean being eternally self-sacrificing. Before you can help anyone else, you need to help yourself. It's simply not sustainable to serve others at the cost of your own healing. Psychologists undergo regular psych evaluations themselves to ensure they're in the right state of mind to help others carry their burdens. Similarly, you need to pour time and energy into your own healing before you can help others heal.

Establish a routine of self-development and self-care for yourself, so you, too, are growing and stay healthy. This self-care needs to extend to all aspects of your being: physical, mental, and spiritual. Life is about a balance between the body, mind, and soul.

Give yourself the time to rest. That is a must if you are to avoid burnout. Deep, regenerative rest in the form of meditation will keep your mind at its best. It's helpful to have a few minutes of deep breathing or meditation before bed; it gives your mind a chance to become quiet and rest. In addition to this, it helps both the mind and the soul to have long nature walks. Always remember that this kind of rest should be a regular part of your routine. Nowadays, it's especially important to stop the relentless digital availability and pull the plug on a regular basis.

When you choose to serve people, you need to be at your best. Taking care of yourself is an expression of your love for humanity, which ultimately includes you as well. Proactively take out the time to look after yourself; you'll find it makes it easier to take care of others as well.

Leading by Example

Did your parents ever tell you to "do as they say, not as they do?"

Do you think that was an effective way of making you listen?

Children are not so different from adults when it comes to the art of learning life lessons. Let's say a father tells his son not to engage in pointless arguments, or to let things go. But then the father spends long hours in fruitless quarrels with his neighbors.

What lesson do you think is being imparted to his young ward? Is it likelier that he will listen to what his father has to say for him, or that he will emulate him? As I've written at the beginning of this book, my father taught me a lot of things simply by doing them. I learned from him to do things with 100% commitment from A to Z, not because he told me, he simply showed me the example.

Some clichés stick around because they are true. Actions are louder than words. This is simply a fact of life, the way things are. No matter how loudly you proclaim morality to the masses, if you do not practice what you preach, you simply won't have any sort of effect. It is a question of integrity.

Therefore, leading by example isn't just the best way to lead; it's the **only** way to lead.

The fact is that there's no need to preach at all.

When you lead a spiritually fulfilling life yourself, the effects of it will manifest themselves to the people around you. What's more, you make it apparent that it is not only possible but healthy and satisfying to live the kind of life you are leading.

That is extremely attractive to the people around you. You then become a guiding beacon that is shining its light for the benefit of others.

That's why you need to live up to your best self on a daily basis. Again, this is something that comes about incrementally. You have to be committed, before you create the best version of yourself in order to reach an abundant life. And in the process, you will transform into a lighthouse that guides others. As Uncle Ben famously tells Spiderman, "With great power comes great responsibility." Similarly, with great progress in your personal life, comes a great responsibility to explore and develop your best self and live up to it every single day.

Why? Because you have a duty to be an example for others and guide them so that they can reach their next level of awareness as well. You can't keep enlightenment to yourself; it's something that shoots out of you and affects the people around you. You need to be the guiding light for someone else.

This is the ultimate purpose of life. It sounds contradictory, but it is what it is; by serving others, you are serving yourself.

Moving From the 3D Way of Living to Quantum Living

Meditation guru Dr. Joe Dispenza has a lot to say about transforming your life from a 3D state (the "Newtonian World") to what he refers to as Quantum living. So, what do these unfamiliar terms mean? Well, to be in a state of 3D consciousness is to have a purely physical perspective. You experience nothing but what your five senses impart to you. You can also refer to this level of consciousness as *I believe what I can see.*

Our rational mind and his co-workers the five senses suggest that only what you can see, touch, smell, hear, or taste really exist. But is that true, or is it not a very limited and even arrogant way of assessing life and the universe. Remember the story of the horses in Vienna wearing the blinkers. Let's try to develop a 360-degree view of life, let go of old convictions, and "be open to everything and attached to nothing."

The 3D way of experiencing life also suggests that you are an individual, completely separate from other people. Life, therefore, becomes a competition. If you're different from others, it means that your needs and wants must take priority over everyone else's. You are constantly assessing your value by comparing yourself with the outer world. That means that the more money you have and the higher your social status, the more "fulfilled" you are. You may be able to find some sort of joy and short-term excitement in a 3D state, but these are shallow and surface-level positives. Plus, they leave you unable to deal with any pain or negative emotions that are buried deep inside of you.

The 3D approach also makes you think that you cannot influence the reality of your existence through your thoughts, meaning whatever you come across is coincidental, not meaningful.

When you live in a 3D state, you feel no desire to introspect or to look for deeper meaning within things. Instead, you skim the surface and get by in life. You remain suspended in a shallow state of being. It is the state when life happens TO you, but not FOR you.

As Joe Dispenza says, mystics have long proclaimed our lived reality to actually be an illusion. In order to proceed beyond this reality, we need to figure out just what reality means, or what we accept it to be.

Our 3D reality is composed of the people we interact with, the places we inhabit, the objects we engage with, and the quality of time. You focus your energy on the areas where you place your attention. So, if all your attention is constantly focused on external elements that cause you stress and emotional imbalance, then you become accustomed to living with that stress. The hormones that stimulate stress cause your senses to be heightened. This will lead to an even narrower focus on material elements such as places, people, objects, and time. And thus, you transform into a materialist who prioritizes material things above all else. You only see the *matter*, not the *energy* lying within.

Additionally, when you constantly remain in a state of stress, you force your body into habitual survival mode. There are very real long-term effects to living under such a prolonged period of stress. One of these is that your capacity to maintain any sort of connection to your inner best self and hence to the energy of the universe is impaired, and thus, you feel separated. You then try to bring about change through the material or matter, but that's just an illusion. Your focus on the material makes you believe that if you can't see something, it simply doesn't exist. But that's just the blind spot materialism causes. If you've focused all your attention and energy in 3D reality, you've forced yourself to change reality by changing matter. So, if you have some sort of problem, you try to eliminate it by affecting the physical causes of it. That's going to take a lot of time.

So what's the solution to this way of thinking? What else is there besides the 3D way of living?

Well, there's always a yin to the yang. Materialism does have an inverse. Dr. Dispenza refers to this as **Quantum Living**. This is when you stop investing your attention and energy into a 3D reality and instead invest it into what is known as "the field," which contains energy, not matter.

Stop paying attention to the material things you own. Don't focus on your own life and body. Forget your identity, and the people and places you know. Leave even the concept of time behind. What are you left with?

Pure consciousness!

When you place your attention into the quantum field, a realm you can't use your senses to experience, you invest your energies to it. You can't physically see this realm; you have to use your own consciousness to become aware of it.

By doing so, you become conscious of energy itself.

And then you try to connect with this energy.

This is the energy that forms matter.

You may think that it is matter that emits the field of energy, but the reality is that it is the other way around. It's the energy that organizes and brings the matter to coherence. This is what brings orderliness and forms structure.

What do you think happens when you connect to this unifying energy?

Wouldn't it transform your life and body, making both of them more organized and structured?

What does this mean for the process of healing or change?

Well, it means that trying to affect matter in order to bring about change is extremely difficult. In order to really bring about change, you need to move beyond the material 3D world and enter what your senses can't see. You need to return to the mothership, so to speak, and stop paying attention to whatever issue it is that you're trying to change. Focus that attention instead of shifting the patterns in the field of energy. As you change that field, you'll project the effects directly onto the 3D reality that you experience with your five senses.

When you try to change matter using matter, you're giving in to the false notion that matter forms the basis of reality. However, the fact is that energy is what underpins the very essence of life and the universe. Therefore, you need to use energy to transform your 3D reality. This makes you a creator instead of just someone who reacts to the change in their lives.

It's normal for most people to spend their lives focusing on what they want from it. And then they go about it in a totally topsy-turvy way, trying to change matter to reach their goals. But there's a lot more to us than mere matter. We are connected to a realm with a wholly different informational fingerprint.

Let's pause here for a while and digest this (probably completely novel) bite. It is tough to accept that there is another reality, or level consciousness, in addition to the one that we are so used to. This has nothing to do with any religious preferences or spiritual convictions. This is pure physics. If you still doubt it, I suggest you go back to chapter "Quantum Physics" on page 79. Even the most convinced sceptic can, at least for a few seconds, allow these ideas to enter into his mind – no risk no fun! Remember what I wrote about the entrance ticket to a limitless amusement park that was given to you right after birth? Now consider that this ticket grants you access to TWO Disney Worlds, instead of only one – what an outlook! Now it is up to you to believe in the existence of the quantum field and tab into it. Is it a scary, uncomfortable thought? Most probably yes, as it is outside of your comfort zone. Now it is a good moment to turn this fear into curiosity, take the key and open the door to the unknown.

We all have the capacity to use this field for the purpose of creating or altering things in the 3D realm. For this, we need to separate ourselves from the material world. And how do we do this? Through meditation, of course.

When we meditate, we dissociate ourselves from our external worlds and our very bodies. We cut the channel that provides us with external impressions, and instead, start the inner journey. By doing so, we open another channel, a channel that connects us to the universal energy field. The field of quantum energy.

Transforming from a 3D to a quantum life is not just a theoretical idea. It's a very real, practical approach to changing your life for the better.

That said, there are some very specific challenges associated with the change. For instance, when people feel that their lives are not transforming fast enough, they are likely to experience frustration, impatience, and anger. This can cause them to become discouraged about using this new method to effect change. And so, they try to force results despite not having the skills or patience to naturally connect with the field of energy. It takes time to learn these skills, so when they try to force an unnatural outcome, it just doesn't pan out.

It can even lead to lying to themselves. They may think they had a vision that connects to a particular outcome without actually having had that vision. They've just had the idea in the 3D realm, and are now perceiving it to be the truth, just because they don't yet have the skills and capacity to create using the field. And so, their lives won't be getting any better. They may be engaging zealously with the philosophy, but they won't actually be able to create any change. Let me remind you here to the compound approach, small but effective action, continuously applied – *haste makes waste.*

Never forget that it is all about a journey, your journey. Declare this journey as your new destination. If you follow this approach, you manage to live more and more in the present time, which is the door towards the quantum world. That's where living by example comes in. Instead of just spouting off the philosophy, we need to embody it by ridding ourselves of the limitations of our physical bodies and environment, and even the time we live in. That's the only way to use the quantum state in order to create change within the material realm.

You need to have a strong connection to the feedback system of the 3D realm in order to effect change. This is where people can become misguided. You may have a dream, or witness a physical happening such as a white bird flying in the sky, and then interpret it as a symbol or a sign of the truth. But that's not real feedback. Actual feedback occurs when things change in a person's life in a way that relates to the area where they have been focusing their attention and their energies. This is when the things that were only true internally manifest themselves into your external reality. When you notice this happening, you'll think about what has changed about your feelings and inner thoughts in order to see that result. That's the feedback system. You cause a change in your 3D reality and then try to see how you did it. Then you do it better. If this reminds you of the Toyota Kata we have discussed before you are absolutely right, it follows the loop "Do – Feedback as need – Adjust." The beauty of the technique is that you combine the best of two worlds. You "Do" it in the Quantum world and get the "Feedback as needed" in the 3D reality so that you get the necessary input to "Adjust" your attention to the next intended outcome. That´s an excellent paradigm of change.

So, what is it that you need to do?

You need to surrender yourself to the outcomes you see.

And you need to learn to remain in the unknown energy field, even if it makes you uncomfortable. You cannot return to your old thoughts and practices just because it's easier. Self-development and hence life happens outside of your comfort zone. You need to learn to keep your heart and your brain coherent within the quantum field so you can maintain your energy levels even when it is challenging or difficult to do so. And finally, you need to learn to associate the changes you make in your inner feelings, thoughts, and behaviors with the outcomes you see in your outer 3D world. This is how you move from the belief that you are at the mercy of life's circumstances to the belief that you are the one who creates them. Consistent feedback is the special sauce that makes this entire process work. That's why you need to practice meditation on a daily basis. Your energy should consistently match the vibration of the energy that you are envisioning. To reach this point, you need to meditate with focus, persistence, and determination.

Of course, there will always also be instances when you will need to influence matter in order to get something done. After all, we still reside within the realm of 3D. However, even these actions are connected with the quantum state of being. When we start to properly create from the quantum state, our life will start to experience little shifts, which, as per the compound effect, will all add up. Those minor shifts are the signs and symbols that will cause a desire within you to return to that quantum field of energy over and over again. You familiarize yourself with that energy, to the extent that it develops a new aspect of your personality. You can see that what you change internally has an effect on your external reality. You've undergone a paradigm shift; you're *causing an effect*. You may think the universe is revolving around you. You may think that the things that happen in your life happen as a result of your understanding, even if you admit to yourself that said understanding is limited. However, you need to move into the unknown quantum state if you are to move beyond this limited understanding and connect to a whole new future. That is when your internal reality starts to manifest itself in your external world. In other words, you start *seeing what you believe*.

Remember, this isn't just a working theory. Moving to the quantum state is something you can practically achieve, and you need to do the work in order to get to this level. It's a deeply pragmatic approach to life that involves embodying the philosophical ideal to its truest extent. As you continue to practice this, you will master the process so that it feels like second nature to you.

Congratulations! You made it (almost) through the whole book. I hope you enjoyed the journey so far. Now, you are ready. Ready to take full responsibility for your life and to contribute to the well-being of others. You have not only (re)built your life, you are also ready to shine a light. As it is an ongoing journey, in this case, being "ready" refers only to this precious moment in the present. If you also want to be ready tomorrow, you better continue "traveling," and to help you in this part of your journey, you might want to have a closer look into the Epilogue.

Epilogue

Back in Chapter 1, I introduced the idea of an obsolete contract.

I couldn't stop thinking about how I, and indeed, everyone else in society, had been shanghaied into signing a contract that defined the terms and conditions I was to follow to be "successful" in life. Society has certain expectations of us, and we've all been fed the idea that if we're to get anywhere in life, we have to live up to these expectations.

We make this agreement for a successful life when we come into the world without any consultation about what we want from life, without a concrete idea what really matters to us. Society is the Leader, and we're all mere Followers.

This contract wants us to commit to applying society's limiting rules for professional success, assuming that with professional success, personal well-being will follow. If we're going to succeed according to the agreement, we need to be "realistic" and avoid far-fetched dreams at all costs. The sparrow in your hand is better than the pigeon on the roof. We have to align with the rules and values of society mindlessly. We need to prioritize math and science at school and study at a well-reputed faculty. Once we pass school, we need to get a master's or a Ph.D. At work, we need to learn to play office politics, applying the written and unwritten rules of the corporate system.

And just what is this professional success such a life will supposedly endow you with? Financial security, social status, health insurance, a nice house, and a big car. That's the most you should expect out of life. Apparently, if you have these, you can be branded a successful individual that the people around you will envy and strive to emulate.

If you're anything like me (and since you've read this entire book and come to the epilogue, I believe you are!), this sounds awful or irritating at the least.

Are you supposed to limit the entirety of your professional career and hence of your private life to these reductive terms and conditions? How can you just view success as nothing more than monetary or material benefits?

As I mentioned back in the Preface, I signed the contract just like others did. I did as society asked of me, and I received paychecks, bonus payments, and pension schemes in return. Both parties were holding up their ends of the contract, but I still felt cheated. This book started out as an attempt to clarify the definition of success in a way that makes sense to me. Success does involve financial achievements to me, but it is far from the most important one. It's about achieving my own goals, not goals that have been thrust on me from above. I created an understanding of what my set of goals and true values are and then developed my personality to make those goals achievable.

My intentions outline my destination, and my values orient me in my journey. And thus, I have formed a new contract with life, one that allows me to live a purposeful, meaningful, and satisfying existence. As we've seen in this book, this has allowed me to transform my way of life and my worldview.

Finally, I did not only review my (now obsolete) contract; no. I even dared to rewrite it based on my own terms and conditions.

So, what does this new contract look like?

The New Contract

In order to live a meaningful life, we need a new contract with society to replace the previous one. The original contract leaves little room for individual needs, subsuming the wide world into a grey mass that cares about nothing but financial success and status. The new contract, however, is a way to insert abundance into your life. It grants you the chance to live on your own terms, not on terms dictated by a faceless society.

How do we go about creating this new contract?

Well, the first step is to combine powerful intentions with elevated levels of emotion, as Dr. Dispenza would say. Intention helps you clarify what you want, so you know what it is that you want to happen. By making an intention, you lay down the foundation of what you want and figure out how to make something greater occur. But the intention's just the first part of making your goals come to life. You have to follow it up by placing yourself in the *energy of creation*.

What does that mean? To make something happen, to create something out of nothing, you need to pair up "a clear intention with an elevated emotion," according to Dr. Dispenza. For this, we need to stay connected to the energy of the goal. We balance our intentions with a touch of surrender, trusting our creation to the organization of the universe. Our connection to this energy heightens and elevates our emotions, allowing our creativity to unfold for us in the right way, even if it's different from the way we imagined it to be. It is the 360-degree view that I suggested explaining the unlimited opportunities life offers to us. These opportunities are not all directly in sight (remember the 3D world, respectively, the blinkers that we are all wearing), instead sometimes we need to let it go and trust that things will fall into places.

Elevating our positive, creation-related emotions also involves putting a lid on negative emotions like frustration, impatience, anger, and resentfulness; these disconnect us from our energies. Why? Because then you're no longer trusting the universe to take you towards the direction of your goals; you're trying to manipulate, predict, control, or force the outcome. Those negative emotions separate us from our goals and creation, keeping us from achieving what we want. Remember, you need to approach a creation as energy changing matter, not as matter organizing matter. Otherwise, you'll simply be back to trying to predict and control how matter transformations are to happen, taking you back to the material, known realm. In order to effect actual change, you need to remain in the unknown realm of energy, even if it makes you uncomfortable to do so. When you try to predict something, you're thinking about a possibility you know about from a past memory and then attempting to bring that outcome into existence in the future. If this does not happen, you experience further feelings of resentment and frustration, thus severing your connection to the energy of your goal.

Feel like you keep doing the work without anything happening? That's your lack of trust within the universe – it's you still attempting to make external forces affect your internal state. But matter takes a long time to change compared to energy. Your external environment will take time to align with your inner world and vision. That's why it's so important to do the work every day, to meditate and remain in your creation's energy. You can't hope, wish, want, or even force your goals into creation. You have to merge with the energy of your goal through meditation and then maintain that energy every day. By staying connected to that energy, we allow our body to memorize until it becomes a natural state of existence for us, means a habit. In this way, you become part of your creation, so it feels like the creation has already occurred. Therefore, it is important to pour all your efforts into staying in the energy of creation.

Practically speaking, how does it feel to visualize yourself, achieving what you want to achieve. How does it feel to be able to play the guitar? How does it feel to win this strategic new client for your business? How does it feel to have this honest, long-time postponed discussion with your parents or partner?

I can share with you how it feels when I visualize myself ordering my book on an e-commerce platform and unpacking it after delivery. It is an emotion of attaining significant achievement, satisfaction, pride, and a huge sense of gratefulness.

"Gratitude is not only the greatest of virtues but the parent of all others."

-Cicero

When you feel and embrace such heightened emotion, you will be inspired by your goals for the future. Thus, you will rewire your brain and body, so that they live in the present instead of the past. Combined with a clear intention, the body, therefore, comes to realize the possibilities of the future. When embracing a new possibility, envision the goals you want to achieve and figure out the choices you'll need to make. Then, review your thoughts and feelings, and practice the changes in behaviour you will need to work on to get the experiences you want. If you really want to create a better future for yourself, one that is all about your goals and not the goals of society, you need to actively envision that future for yourself.

Otherwise, you will still be stuck in the past, unable to move forward and create what you want. When we combine an elevated emotion with an open heart and a conscious intention with clear thought, we signal the field, preparing it to respond in amazing ways. The quantum field does not respond to what we want; it responds to *who we are becoming*. What does all of this has to do with a new contract? Well, when you're creating this new contract, you should have clarity about all your intentions, and the emotions linked to each intention. Start writing your own contract here. Based on my experience, it is not so easy to work with your emotions. Indeed I needed to confront myself with a list of positive emotional states first before I could allow myself to feel the different intentions. On my web page, <yourlighhousejourney.com>, you can find a contract template as well as the list of positive emotions for your own use. You can also send me an email to dirk.sanden@yourlighthousejourney.com to get the original files, or in case you want to discuss this further.

Last but not least, please note that this new contract is not set in stone. It is rather a living document that should be reviewed by yourself, at least, on an annual basis. Life is moving fast. Hence, your definition of a successful life worth living might also change. Yesterday, it was maybe your intention to stop judging other people, today it is being more mindful and live in the present moment, and tomorrow? Everything together and a lot more…

As a little piece of inspiration, you can find my new contract below.

AGREEMENT FOR AN ABUNDANT & JOYFUL LIFE

THIS AGREEMENT is made and entered into this September 17th, 2019 by and between Dirk Sanden hereinafter referred to as "LEADER" and the society, hereinafter referred to as "FOLLOWER."

1. The parties agree that the follower will offer a world of unlimited opportunities, listed in paragraph 2, and the leader promises to dive into this sea of unlimited opportunities, develops his best self, live up to it on a daily basis and cast a light for others as further described in paragraph 3.

2. The world of UNLIMITED OPPORTUNITIES

a. A universe that offers a friendly environment in which kindness is the ultimate measure for success.

b. Freedom of thought and free will.

c. An open community that is supportive and looking for some support itself.

d. Guidance on how to discover your very own special talent.

e. A work environment that follows a "people first"

business philosophy.

f. Relatives and friends that are caring for you, without expecting any return.

g. An environment in which unconditional love is the overarching principle.

h. A Non-judgemental society that facilitates authenticity.

i. An ocean of limitless energy.

3. The LEADERS´ RESPONSIBILITY

a. Focus your mind on the above-listed framework.

b. Get rid of your blinkers and limiting beliefs and dive into this ocean of unlimited opportunities.

c. Trust the universe in the moment of doubt.

d. Explore your best self and live up to it on a daily basis.

e. Be yourself, without any exception.

f. Get clarity on what really matters to you and why you have your boots on the ground.

g. Develop a sustainable mind by thinking of sustainable thoughts.

h. Be of service and offer your helping hand

unconditionally.

i. Shine a light for others to guide them toward an abundant life.

<u>Strassen/Luxembourg (place)</u>, <u>September 17th, 2019 (date)</u>

_*Dirk Sanden* _ _ *The Society* _

(Signature)   (Signature)

The Leader   The Follower

Leadership – A View from the Inside

Why is it so important that you figure out how to achieve your goals, what really matters to you, and getting clarity about the purpose of your existence? Because once you understand how to be successful on your own terms, you're ready to lead other people to success as well. To be a good leader, you need to first clean your own doorsteps. That's why personal development is a key component of any leadership training, and that principle applies to this book as well.

To witness success in your career, organization, relationships, or life in general, you need to have effective leadership skills. And to be a good leader, you need to develop yourself, constantly. Personal development is something that you incorporate into your very nature; it's not just something that you practice and then put away. It has to become an indelible part of you. Good leaders invest in their own development. This takes time and effort, as you expose yourself to different facets of life, and learn to deal with the unexpected twists and turns in your way. But it also involves sticking to your core values and beliefs and developing the mindset and worldview to achieve the goals you have envisioned for yourself. One hallmark of a good leader is an insatiable appetite for personal development and learning. Good leaders cannot stop learning and are always trying to understand how to best reach their goals. They take actions that help them learn new and innovative techniques, no matter what. At the same time, they create a balance between their body, mind, and soul.

Good leaders understand that there is no such thing as work-life balance; there is only a life balance. In fact, they understand that success doesn't just come in the form of material wealth and financial achievements; success also includes mental stability, healthy relationships, and a sense of peace.

Leaders also need to be strongly self-disciplined. They need to stick to their values and moral standards, despite the constant temptation to cut ethical corners. For a great leader, integrity is key. As a leader, you need to be a passionate agent of positive change, constantly looking to grow and develop yourself and inspiring the people around you to formulate and achieve their own goals as well. Work on yourself, so you play to your strengths and further improve them. You also need to overcome the conditioning of your past and understand that you don't have to go by society's dictation. In this way, you make choices that lead you to success on your terms, changing your behaviours, habits, and attitudes accordingly. Act with integrity and sound values.

Here are some of the ways you can work on your personal development.

Identify your goals so that you can work towards them tangibly. Write them down or put up representations of them on a vision board, so you are constantly reminded of them. Work on achieving these goals by aligning your internal energy with your vision of what you want from your future. Then learn to overcome the obstacles in the way of your goal. These obstacles don't just arise from your external environment but are likelier to be a result of your internal state. Your negative emotions, such as impatience, frustration, and anger, inhibit you, and keep you from surrendering to the power of the energy field. While you shouldn't try to force or predict an outcome, it helps to envision and anticipate your vision. This practice helps you keep motivated.

What else helps personal development? Well, you should start the practice of reading voraciously on a variety of topics. As a leader, you need to expand your base of knowledge and give yourself further opportunities for creativity, innovation, and new approaches to solving problems. The more perspectives you acquaint yourself with, the more open and receptive your mind will be to new ideas and concepts, as well as novel ways to reach your goals.

It also helps to spend a good portion of your time in self-reflection and thinking. Leave your phones and laptops behind, and make time for yourself to think and reflect on your goals and to plan out your day. This lack of distraction is something that is sorely missing from the fast-paced routines of modern life, and it keeps us from having any time at all to ourselves.

At the same time, don't let your eyes wander from your broader goals for success. You need to be laser-focused on what you really want to achieve so you can work towards living your life just the way you want. As the previous paragraph said, it's a fast-paced life, and it can get hectic and overwhelming at the drop of a hat. Sometimes, you need to make quick decisions, and if you're not entirely in sync with your intentions and believes, you could easily make a mistake and deviate from the vision you have for your future. Maintain a clear connection to your goals and vision; your intention should always remain strong. By doing so, you will be less likely to make decisions or act out behaviours that increase the distance between you and your vision.

You should also maintain a healthy sense of curiosity about the wider world, other people, and even yourself. You don't know what your capacities, limitations, and quirks are until you delve into your psyche and discover truths about yourself. In the same manner, you should be curious about how other people think or approach tasks; this can give you valuable insights into your development. Additionally, it's important to have a keen understanding of how the people around you perceive you. While you do need to stay connected to your internal self, feedback from others is a valuable tool in self-improvement. So, maybe going forward, you want to speak less and listen more.

In that vein, you should always be ready to be wrong. This can be harder for some than others. It's not always easy to admit that you've been wrong, but it's important that you inculcate the ability to be objective when considering other points of view. When leading people, make sure you leave them the space to engage in healthy debate with you. It's easier said than done, especially when you're extremely passionate about your vision and goals. But if you see evidence that's contrary to what you believe in, you need to confront it, and even be open to the possibility of changing your mind. It takes a great deal of practice and work to be an effective leader, even when you have been blessed with natural leadership ability.

Whether you're planning on leading the people around you someday, or you have decades of experience with leading, you cannot put a stop to honing your leadership skills. When you stop learning, you stop growing. As we've learned in this book, morning intentions are an excellent way to keep yourself charged and motivated throughout the day. Apply morning intentions and affirmations to all your goals, including the one for self-improvement. After you open your eyes in the morning, take five minutes to set an intention for what you will do in the day, and another for the state of mind you will be in. Connect your goals with the required energy levels and mindset in order to remain focused on your task of personal development.

Practice mindfulness. We've talked about this a lot in this book, but the topic is well worth another visit. Mindfulness is an art that you can employ in order to optimize your well-being and your ability to reach your goals. It lets you enjoy meaningful professional success alongside a peaceful and fulfilling life. When you practice mindfulness, you are able to impact all aspects of your life. Leaders can therefore develop relationships that are positive and mutually beneficial.

Through personal development, you will attain the tools you require to succeed in both your personal and professional lives. Develop yourself in order to accomplish more than you were once able to.

Becoming a Better Leader through Mindfulness

Mindfulness, as described in this book, is an excellent technique to develop yourself into a better leader. Meditation, a key aspect of mindfulness, especially helps you develop a sense of well-being and lets you focus on what actually matters. It also gives you more clarity when it comes to decision-making. Many leaders have also experienced an increased frequency of creative ideas after meditation.

After all, when you train your mind during meditation, you actually transform the very biological composition of your brain. This is verified by research conducted by Richard Davidson from Wisconsin, who revealed a direct relationship between mindfulness and alterations in the brain that lead it away from anxiety and anger and towards peace and calm. What's more, the Mindful Awareness Research Centre at UCLA has demonstrated meditation's ability to improve executive functions by decreasing the brain's capacity for distraction and increasing its ability to sustain attention.

The practice of mindfulness helps the brain achieve a state that eases leadership. After all, it decreases stress levels, improves sleep quality, and reduces pain. Together, these little effects serve to improve your focus and ability to lead others. It helps leaders showcase attributes like intentionality in their actions, and makes them more self-aware. It also instills in them the crucial leadership qualities of courage, compassion, and passion.

Let's talk about some of the leadership qualities mindfulness helps you gain.

Self-awareness: Most people go about their daily lives, unaware of their emotional state and how others perceive them. They are missing that necessary quality of self-awareness, and thus cannot attain completeness of knowledge regarding their own personhoods. The practice of mindfulness can facilitate self-awareness, which is an essential quality for leaders. You need to be aware of your behaviours if you are to ensure that you are the person and Leader you want to be. You may conceptually know what your ideal self looks like – the behaviours that will help you reach your goals and make you the Leader you want to be. But do you know how much distance you have to cover to get to this ideal state? To attain this knowledge, you need the ability to objectively and continuously compare your present reality with the ideal you have envisioned.

Your self-awareness leads to emotional intelligence, which enables you to perceive yourself as other people do. It helps you understand how your words and actions directly or indirectly impact others. This is vital for you to comprehend the kind of impact you have on others, and the impression you create on your followers.

The ability to be present at the moment: With the myriad distractions and complexities of modern life, it's no surprise how hard it is to be truly present in the moment. Maintaining focus without being side-tracked is difficult when the world wants you to focus on ten different things at the same time. That's where mindfulness comes in. It helps you pay attention to the goals that are actually important to you, as opposed to the goals society expects you to achieve. Mindfulness allows you to focus on the actual purpose of the actions that you undertake, and to prioritize them according to your values. Through mindfulness, you stop spending your time worrying about the things you have to do and instead focus on what you are currently doing in the here and now.

Compassion: You can't be a leader without compassion and empathy. When you want to lead the people around you and help them achieve their goals for the future, you need to understand that their visions will not necessarily be the same as yours. Therefore, they might not even take the same path as you to get to their goals. This doesn't mean that you should discount them or treat them with anything less than kindness. Then there will be the people that find it difficult to skip out on society's obsolete contract altogether. You need to marshal up your reserves of compassion and kindness for them as well and avoid getting impatient or frustrated with them. Negative emotions do nothing but scare people away from your goal. Through mindfulness, you can develop the kind of understanding and patience you need to be compassionate and engage with people.

Resilience: A leader needs to be able to cope with stress and bear the pressure of setbacks. Stress can cause you to make mistakes, lose focus, and become distracted, or beat yourself up for not achieving your goals fast enough. Mindfulness can help you deal with the stress you feel when you're ineffectively trying to accomplish all your goals all at once. It helps you block out any irrelevant information and gives perspective and context on what you're trying to achieve. This eliminates stress and helps you become a more resilient leader.

If you're invested in becoming a leader, you need to start practicing mindfulness now. Keep at the practice with discipline and grit. It's not easy to make this a part of your routine, but you need to stick to it and make acts of mindful introspection, something you do daily. Slowly, you'll find yourself worrying less about run-of-the-mill problems and start focusing on the goals and vision you have set for yourself. And as you live up to your own set of values and principles, you'll see that other people will begin looking up to you as an example. "If they can do it, maybe I can too!" That is how you become a leader; by being the type of person that others want to follow. As you become a more mindful person, you will grow to become a more fulfilled, successful, and effective leader.

Before You Can Be an Effective Leader, You First Have to Lead Yourself

To be an effective leader, you have to lead by example. That's why it's so important that you improve yourself first.

As someone who has broken away from society's contract to make your own, you are at the forefront of a movement that prioritizes unique individual needs and goals over those that benefit no one but corporations. Once you have achieved this level of existence, you will feel the need to be of service to the people around you. You will want to lead them out of their stagnant way of being so they too can achieve their goals and define their own standard of success. But you can only do so if you are a living embodiment of the ideals that you espouse.

If you encourage people to leave behind society's static rules in favour of carving out their path but fail to live up to your values and goals, you will never be able to effectively motivate them to change their lives for the better. Why should they listen to you, after all? You're not even listening to yourself!

Ensure you're always setting the example that you want to see in others. For this, you need to be intimately acquainted with your principles and values, and connected to the energy of the creation of your goals. Otherwise, you are not in a position to lead yourself, let alone others. Never forget that integrity, and hence doing the right thing, is key.

Leadership is a process that starts with yourself. That's why it's so important to invest in yourself. You may have some natural leadership traits, but you need to hone both your knowledge and skills through grit and determination. The finest athlete in the world can't skip out on practice and honing their natural talents, and neither should you.

Congratulations on making it through to the end of this book! From ditching an obsolete contract to making a new one for yourself, from creating your own set of unique values and goals to developing the mindset and worldview that will help you achieve them, from leading yourself to leading others, this will be the ride of your life. It's a long way up the lighthouse, but the journey is well worth it.

Be the LIGHT for others, take good care of your own HOUSE, and enjoy the JOURNEY.

Bibliography

McCarty, R. Atkinson, M. Stolc, V. Alabdulgader, A.A. Vainoras, A. Ragulskis, M. (2017). Synchronization of Human Autonomic Nervous System Rhythms with Geomagnetic Activity in Human Subjects. MDPI. Retrieved from: https://www.mdpi.com/1660-4601/14/7/770

Der Linden, SV (2013). The Helper's High. Princeton. Retrieved from: https://scholar.princeton.edu/sites/default/files/slinden/files/helpershigh.pdf

Castillo, S (2012). 13 Ways to Be Nicer. Prevention. Retrieved from: https://www.prevention.com/life/a20447046/doing-kind-acts-reduces-anxiety-study/

United Health Group (2013). Doing Good is Good for You. Retrieved from: https://www.unitedhealthgroup.com/content/dam/UHG/PDF/2013/UNH-Health-Volunteering-Study.pdf

United Health Group (2013). Doing Good is Good for You. Retrieved from: https://www.unitedhealthgroup.com/content/dam/UHG/PDF/2013/UNH-Health-Volunteering-Study.pdf

Harvard Health Publishing (2019). Giving thanks can make you happier. Retrieved from:

https://www.health.harvard.edu/healthbeat/giving-thanks-can-make-you-happier

Alex M. Wood, Maltby, J. Joseph, S. (2008). Gratitude uniquely predicts satisfaction with life: Incremental validity above the domains and facets of the five-factor model. Science Direct. Retrieved from: https://www.health.harvard.edu/healthbeat/giving-thanks-can-make-you-happier

Ed De Costa (2012). Believing is seeing: Self-confidence in action. Retrieved from: https://eddecosta.com/believing-is-seeing-self-confidence-in-action/

DIRK SANDEN